빵빵GO!

초판 제1쇄   **2024년 9월 1일**

저자	서장혁
펴낸이	서장혁
편집	토마토출판사 편집부
표지디자인	이새봄
본문디자인	이새봄
주소	서울 마포구 양화로 161 727호
TEL	1544-5383
홈페이지	www.tomato4u.com
E-mail	support@tomato4u.com
등록	2012.1.11.
ISBN	979-11-92603-61-2 14740

미국 3살 아이들은
문법도 모르는데
어떻게 영어를 잘 할까?

미국인의 영어 습득 과정은 우리의 한국어 습득 과정과 똑같습니다.
문법이나, 단어 암기와 상관없이 어릴 때부터 부모와 소통하는데 쓰인
표현이 익숙해지다 보면 각 상황에 맞춰 그 표현이 자연스럽게 본인의
의사 전달 수단이 되는 것입니다.

그럼, 우리도
미국 3살 아이들이 습득했던 방식으로
영어를 할 수 있을까?

국내에서 단지 영어 공부만 열심히 한다고 해서 미국 아이들처럼 영어를
말하기란 쉽지 않습니다.
가장 중요한 요소는 공부가 아니라 24시간 동안 내가 얼마나 영어로 소
통할 수 있는 환경에 있는가 하는 것입니다.

'빵빵GO' 프로그램은 국내 학습자들이
24시간 영어 환경에 노출되도록 하는 것이
목표입니다.

1단계   그냥 24시간 틀어두세요.

외울 필요도, 이해할 필요도 없습니다.
스스로 하루 종일 시간 날 때마다 틀어두세요.
어느 새 미국 3살 아이들처럼 간단한 회화 문장은
바로 영어로 나오게 될 것입니다.
'회화 표현 + 발음 교정 + 리스닝' 동시에 효과를 보실 수 있습니다.

2단계   Random 테스트를 해보세요.

우리의 어학 환경은 정해져 있지 않습니다.
다양한 상황에서도 머리 속에서 이해 과정을 거치지 않고
언제든 자동적으로 말이 나오는지 스스로 확인하세요.

한국인이 가장 혼동하는
1형식, 2형식 회화 문장부터
시작합니다.

이런 분들이 공부하시면 좋아요

**시간 나실 때마다
무조건 틀어 놓으세요!**

1 영어회화를 마땅히 배울 곳이 없는
어린 자녀분들.

2 영어 문법이 어려워
늘 회화도 엄두가 안 났던 분들.

3 배운 회화 문장으로도
현지에서 의사 소통에 애를 먹었던 분들.

4 학원이나 인강에서 강의를 들을 시간조차
나지 않는 직장인 분들.

5 자녀들의 영어 질문에
답하기 곤란했던 학부모 분들.

6 지금 막 해외여행을
계획하고 계신 분들.

'일빵빵'을
공부하실 수 있는 방법 2가지!

1. '교재' 구입 시 언제 어디서나 해당 강의를 즐기실 수 있습니다.

교재를 구입하신 후 가지고 계신 핸드폰으로 각 강의마다 Q.R 코드를 찍으시면 언제 어디서나 해당 영상 강의를 시청하실 수 있습니다.

- 해당 채널의 유튜브 강의는 Q.R코드로만 진행됩니다.
  Q.R 코드가 없는 교재일 경우는 전체 공개 강의입니다.
  유튜브에서 '일빵빵'을 검색하세요.

일빵빵 Q.R

2. '렛츠일빵빵 어플'에서 일빵빵 전체 강의를 즐기실 수 있습니다.

렛츠일빵빵 어플을 다운받으신 후 월 결제 혹은 연 결제로 사용하시면 2천 여개가 수록되어 있는 일빵빵 왕초보부터 기초 심화 단계까지의 모든 강의를 모두 즐기실 수 있습니다.

- 렛츠일빵빵 어플 '이벤트 결제' 시, 시판되고 있는 해당 일빵빵 교재 전체 무료 대량 증정 이벤트가 있으니 놓치지 마세요!
  (결제 금액과 맞먹는 금액의 교재 제공/이벤트 기간 확인 필수)

Let's

렛츠일빵빵 어플

CONTENTS

PART 2.
2형식 동사로 시작하는 회화 문장

빵빵GO! 를 시작하면서

10여 년이 넘는 기간 동안 다양한 학습자 분들을 만났는데

결국 공통적으로 하시는 말씀이

'좀 더 일찍 영어 공부를 했더라면'이었습니다.

네, 맞습니다.

어학은 한 살이라도 어릴 때 학습하는 것이 효과가 큽니다.

이미 성인이 된 후에는 스펀지같이 받아들이기 전에

자꾸 '왜'라는 질문이 앞서기 때문입니다.

이 기회에 한국어를 처음 배웠을 때처럼

어린 나이로 돌아가 보는 것은 어떨까요?

'빵빵GO'를 통해서 3살, 스펀지 같을 때로 다시 돌아가 봅시다.

이제부터 '왜'를 버리세요.

준비되셨죠?

2024년 저자 서장혁 올림

1형식 동사로 시작하는 회화 문장

1. 'go'를 활용한 회화 문장

001	**어떻게 지내?** How's it going?
002	**(그 일/그거) 어땠어?** How did it go?
003	**(하던 거) 계속해.** Go ahead.
004	**가야 할 시간이야.** It's time to go.
005	**(엘리베이터) 올라가요.** Going up.
006	**(엘리베이터) 내려가요.** Going down.
007	**이제 가야 해.** I have to go now.
008	**(전화, 하던 일 중간에) 그만 해야겠다.** I gotta go.
009	**나 안 갈 거야.** I'm not going.
010	**뭐 좀 가져올게.** I'll go get some.

011	가자. Let's go.
012	그냥 가. Just go.
013	저리 가. Go away.
014	가서 앉아 있어. Go sit down.
015	(우리) 어디 가는 거야? Where are we going?
016	자러 갈게. I'm going to bed.
017	해봐. (혹은 화이팅) Go for it.
018	가서 그거 가져와. Go get it.
019	가서 이메일 좀 체크해. Go check your email.
020	너 먼저 가. You can go first.

021	하던 거 계속해. Go on.	☐
022	이야기 계속해. Go on with your story.	☐
023	밖에 나가. Go outside.	☐
024	계속 직진해. Go straight ahead.	☐
025	무슨 일이야? What's going on?	☐
026	분위기 왜 이래? What's going on here?	☐
027	그건 어디 갔어? Where did it go?	☐
028	(너) 어디 갔었어? Where did you go?	☐
029	그 사람 벌써 갔어? Did he go yet?	☐
030	넌 왜 안 가? Why don't you go?	☐

031	너랑 같이 갈게.	
	I'll go with you.	☐

032	잘 됐어.	
	It went well.	☐

033	가서 손 씻어.	
	Go wash your hands.	☐

034	그는 늦을 거야.	
	He's going to be late.	☐

035	너 가야 해.	
	You should go.	☐

036	가고 싶지 않아.	
	I don't want to go.	☐

037	같이 갈 수 있어.	
	We can go together.	☐

038	나가볼게.	
	I'll go out.	☐

039	(우리) 지금 갈 수 있어?	
	Can we go now?	☐

040	돌아가자.	
	Let's go back.	☐

041	가서 간식 먹어.	
	Go grab a snack.	☐
042	방에 가 있어.	
	Go to your room.	☐
043	비가 올 거야.	
	It's going to rain.	☐
044	(너희들) 자야 돼요.	
	You need to go to bed.	☐
045	거기 가지 마.	
	Don't go there.	☐
046	집에 가고 싶어.	
	I want to go home.	☐
047	어젯밤에 검토했어.	
	I went over it last night.	☐
048	(메뉴 선정) 그걸로 할게요.	
	I'll go with that.	☐
049	다시 잠들었어.	
	I went back to sleep.	☐
050	너랑 같이 갈 수 있어?	
	Can I go with you?	☐

| 051 | 산책하러 가자. |
| | Let's go for a walk. ☐ |

| 052 | 쇼핑하러 가자. |
| | Let's go shopping. ☐ |

| 053 | 걔네들 휴가 갔어. |
| | They went on vacation. ☐ |

| 054 | 아빠한테 물어봐. |
| | Go ask your father. ☐ |

| 055 | 엄마가 위층으로 가셨어. |
| | My mom went upstairs. ☐ |

| 056 | 첫째 날인데 어땠어? |
| | How's your first day going? ☐ |

| 057 | 우리 엉뚱한 데로 갔어. |
| | We went wrong somewhere. ☐ |

| 058 | 가서 커피 좀 만들어봐. |
| | Go make some coffee. ☐ |

| 059 | 너 나중에 갈 수 있어? |
| | Can you go later? ☐ |

| 060 | 가서 그녀에게 말 걸어봐. |
| | Go talk to her. ☐ |

| 061 | 걔네들 어젯밤 외출했어. |
| | They went out last night. □ |

| 062 | 어서 드세요. |
| | Go ahead and eat. □ |

| 063 | 나 의사에게 갔었어. |
| | I went to the doctor. □ |

| 064 | 가서 간식 좀 사올게. |
| | I'll go grab some snacks. □ |

| 065 | 걔네들 어디로 가는 거야? |
| | Where are they going? □ |

| 066 | 우리 제대로 가고 있는 거야? |
| | Are we going the right way? □ |

| 067 | 가서 친구들 데리고 와. |
| | Go bring your friends. □ |

| 068 | 가서 좀 쉬어. |
| | Go get some rest. □ |

| 069 | 가서 옷 갈아입고 와. |
| | Go get changed. □ |

| 070 | 피자 먹으러 가자. |
| | Let's go get pizza. |

| 071 | 영화 보러 가자. |
| | Let's go see a movie. | ☐ |

| 072 | 우리 여행 갈 거야. |
| | We're going on a trip. | ☐ |

| 073 | 코트 가져와. |
| | Go get your coat. | ☐ |

| 074 | 네가 먼저 가. |
| | You should go first. | ☐ |

| 075 | 우리 많은 일을 겪었어. |
| | We went through a lot. | ☐ |

| 076 | 괜찮을 거야. |
| | It's going to be okay. | ☐ |

| 077 | 갈 수 있으면 좋겠어. |
| | I wish I could go. | ☐ |

| 078 | 가서 침대 정리해. |
| | Go make your bed. | ☐ |

| 079 | 가서 방 청소해. |
| | Go clean your room. | ☐ |

| 080 | 그가 전화할 거야. |
| | He's going to call. | ☐ |

081	밥 먹으러 가자. Let's go eat.	☐
082	그녀는 화낼 거야. She's going to be upset.	☐
083	가서 밖에서 놀아. Go play outside.	☐
084	브런치 먹으러 가자. Let's go for brunch.	☐
085	운동하러 갈 거야. I'm going to work out.	☐
086	가서 불 좀 꺼. Go turn off the lights.	☐
087	가서 의자 가져와. Go grab a chair.	☐
088	가서 문 닫아. Go shut the door.	☐
089	가서 친구들하고 놀아. Go play with your friends.	☐
090	가서 리모트 가져와 Go bring me the remote.	☐

| 091 | 쇼핑몰에 가자. |
| | Let's go to the mall. □ |

| 092 | 커피 마시러 가자. |
| | Let's go for coffee. □ |

| 093 | 등산하러 가자. |
| | Let's go hiking. □ |

| 094 | 가서 네 형 찾아봐. |
| | Go find your brother. □ |

| 095 | 길을 따라 가. |
| | Go down the street. □ |

| 096 | 같이 가도 돼? |
| | Can we go together? □ |

| 097 | 나랑 같이 갈래? |
| | Will you go with me? □ |

| 098 | 어디까지 갔어? |
| | How far did you go? □ |

| 099 | 지금 갈까, 나중에 갈까? |
| | Should I go now or later? □ |

| 100 | 오늘 저녁에 나랑 데이트 할래? |
| | Will you go out with me tonight? □ |

Check	
☐	**산책하러 가자.** Let's go for a walk.
☐	**브런치 먹으러 가자.** Let's go for brunch.
☐	**커피 마시러 가자.** Let's go for coffee.
☐	**쇼핑몰에 가자.** Let's go to the mall.
☐	**쇼핑하러 가자.** Let's go shopping.
☐	**등산하러 가자.** Let's go hiking.
☐	**가서 그거 가져와.** Go get it.
☐	**가서 앉아 있어.** Go sit down.
☐	**하던 거 계속해.** Go on.
☐	**이야기 계속해.** Go on with your story.

Check		
☐	**첫째 날인데 어땠어?**	How's your first day going?
☐	**가서 손 씻어.**	Go wash your hands.
☐	**가서 간식 먹어.**	Go grab a snack.
☐	**방에 가 있어.**	Go to your room.
☐	**거기 가지 마.**	Don't go there.
☐	**어떻게 지내?**	How's it going?
☐	**자러 갈게.**	I'm going to bed.
☐	**(너희들) 자야 돼요.**	You need to go to bed.
☐	**아빠한테 물어봐.**	Go ask your father.
☐	**엄마가 위층으로 가셨어.**	My mom went upstairs.

☐	**걔네들 어디로 가는 거야?** Where are they going?
☐	**우리 제대로 가고 있는 거야?** Are we going the right way?
☐	**(하던 거) 계속해.** Go ahead.
☐	**어서 드세요.** Go ahead and eat.
☐	**밖에 나가.** Go outside.
☐	**오늘 저녁에 나랑 데이트 할래?** Will you go out with me tonight?
☐	**나가볼게.** I'll go out.
☐	**같이 갈 수 있어.** We can go together.
☐	**(우리) 지금 갈 수 있어?** Can we go now?
☐	**그는 늦을 거야.** He's going to be late.

Check	**가서 그녀에게 말 걸어봐.**
	Go talk to her.
Check	**무슨 일이야?**
	What's going on?
Check	**분위기 왜 이래?**
	What's going on here?
Check	**너랑 같이 갈게.**
	I'll go with you.
Check	**나랑 같이 갈래?**
	Will you go with me?
Check	**(엘리베이터) 올라가요.**
	Going up.
Check	**(엘리베이터) 내려가요.**
	Going down.
Check	**가자.**
	Let's go.
Check	**그냥 가.**
	Just go.
Check	**저리 가.**
	Go away.

	돌아가자. Let's go back.
	너 나중에 갈 수 있어? Can you go later?
	걔네들 어젯밤 외출했어. They went out last night.
	가서 이메일 좀 체크해. Go check your email.
	뭐 좀 가져올게. I'll go get some.
	해봐. (혹은 화이팅) Go for it.
	그건 어디 갔어? Where did it go?
	(너) 어디 갔었어? Where did you go?
	이제 가야 해. I have to go now.
	네가 먼저 가. You should go first.

Check ☐	**가서 침대 정리해.** Go make your bed.
Check ☐	**가서 방 청소해.** Go clean your room.
Check ☐	**가서 친구들 데리고 와.** Go bring your friends.
Check ☐	**가서 좀 쉬어.** Go get some rest.
Check ☐	**가서 옷 갈아입고 와.** Go get changed.
Check ☐	**가서 커피 좀 만들어봐.** Go make some coffee.
Check ☐	**코트 가져와.** Go get your coat.
Check ☐	**(그 일/그거) 어땠어?** How did it go?
Check ☐	**나 안 갈 거야.** I'm not going.
Check ☐	**넌 왜 안 가?** Why don't you go?

☐	**피자 먹으러 가자.** Let's go get pizza.
☐	**영화 보러 가자.** Let's go see a movie.
☐	**가서 간식 좀 사올게.** I'll go grab some snacks.
☐	**그녀는 화낼 거야.** She's going to be upset.
☐	**가서 불 좀 꺼.** Go turn off the lights.
☐	**가서 의자 가져와.** Go grab a chair.
☐	**가서 문 닫아.** Go shut the door.
☐	**나 의사에게 갔었어.** I went to the doctor.
☐	**너 가야 해.** You should go.
☐	**다시 잠들었어.** I went back to sleep.

	밥 먹으러 가자.	Let's go eat.
	우리 엉뚱한 데로 갔어.	We went wrong somewhere.
	우리 여행 갈 거야.	We're going on a trip.
	비가 올 거야.	It's going to rain.
	집에 가고 싶어.	I want to go home.
	가야 할 시간이야.	It's time to go.
	(전화, 하던 일 중간에) 그만 해야겠다.	I gotta go.
	(우리) 어디 가는 거야?	Where are we going?
	갈 수 있으면 좋겠어.	I wish I could go.
	그가 전화할 거야.	He's going to call.

Check	
☐	**가서 밖에서 놀아.** Go play outside.
☐	**길을 따라 가.** Go down the street.
☐	**계속 직진해.** Go straight ahead.
☐	**가서 리모트 가져와.** Go bring me the remote.
☐	**지금 갈까, 나중에 갈까?** Should I go now or later?
☐	**잘 됐어.** It went well.
☐	**어젯밤에 검토했어.** I went over it last night.
☐	**너랑 같이 갈 수 있어?** Can I go with you?
☐	**같이 가도 돼?** Can we go together?
☐	**가고 싶지 않아.** I don't want to go.

Check	
☐	**괜찮을 거야.** It's going to be okay.
☐	**우리 많은 일을 겪었어.** We went through a lot.
☐	**운동하러 갈 거야.** I'm going to work out.
☐	**어디까지 갔어?** How far did you go?
☐	**가서 친구들하고 놀아.** Go play with your friends.
☐	**가서 네 형 찾아봐.** Go find your brother.
☐	**너 먼저 가.** You can go first.
☐	**그 사람 벌써 갔어?** Did he go yet?
☐	**(메뉴 선정) 그걸로 할게요.** I'll go with that.
☐	**걔네들 휴가 갔어.** They went on vacation.

2. 'work / matter / last'를 활용한 회화 문장

101	**잘 돼요.** It works.
102	**매번 잘 돼요.** It works every time.
103	**전혀 안 돼요.** It never works.
104	**어떻게 하는 거예요?** How does it work?
105	**그거 될까요?** Will it work?
106	**안 돼요.** It doesn't work.
107	**지금 안 되는데요.** It's not working.
108	**지금 안 되나요?** Isn't it working?
109	**(식당) 아직 먹고 있어요.** I'm working on it.
110	**(식당) 아직 드시고 계세요?** Are you still working on it?

111	이게 제일 잘 돼요.
	This works best.
112	아직도 돼요?
	Does it still work?
113	배터리로 작동하나요?
	Can it work on battery?
114	작동 가능해요.
	It's workable.
115	(일정) 이 일정 나한테 괜찮아요.
	This works for me.
116	(일정) 그 일정 당신에게 괜찮으시겠어요?
	Would that work for you?
117	(일정) 월요일 날 괜찮아요.
	Monday works for me.
118	그렇게는 안 될 거야.
	That's not going to work.
119	저는 마케팅 팀에서 일해요.
	I work in the Marketing team.
120	그녀는 너무 많이 일해.
	She works too much.

121	일하러 가야 해.	
	I'm off to work.	
122	지금 일하러 가.	
	I'm heading to work.	
123	이거 열심히 했어.	
	I worked hard on this.	
124	아직 일하는 중이야.	
	I'm still at work.	
125	일 시작하자.	
	Let's get to work.	
126	일이 바빠.	
	Work's been busy.	
127	나는 재택 해.	
	I work from home.	
128	그는 열심히 일하고 있어.	
	He's hard at work.	
129	오늘은 일 쉬어요.	
	I'm taking work off today.	
130	점심시간에도 계속 일했어.	
	I worked through lunch.	

131	내일 일해?
	Are you working tomorrow?
132	나는 매일 일해.
	I work every day.
133	오늘 밤 늦게까지 일해야 해.
	I'm working late tonight.
134	그들은 잘 어울려.
	They work well together.
135	수고하세요.
	Keep up the good work.
136	수고가 많으세요.
	You're doing great work.
137	내가 제대로 해볼게. (work on)
	I'll work on that.
138	제대로 좀 해봐. (work on)
	You need to work on it.
139	그들이 제대로 일하기 시작했어. (work on)
	They started working on it.
140	저희가 해결하겠습니다. (work out)
	We'll work it out.

141	일이 잘 안 풀려. (work out)
	It's not working out.
142	중요해요.
	It matters.
143	정말 중요해.
	It really matters.
144	매우 중요해.
	It matters a lot.
145	갑자기 문제가 됐어.
	It suddenly mattered.
146	예전에는 많이 중요했어.
	It used to matter a lot.
147	상관없어.
	It doesn't matter.
148	지금은 중요하지 않아.
	It doesn't matter now.
149	더 이상 중요하지 않아.
	It doesn't matter anymore.
150	그때는 중요하지 않았어.
	It didn't matter then.

151	중요한가요?
	Does it matter?
152	당신에게 중요한가요?
	Does it matter to you?
153	왜 중요한가요?
	Why does it matter?
154	얼마나 중요한가요?
	How much does it matter?
155	무엇이 당신에게 중요한가요?
	What matters to you?
156	그에게는 중요해.
	It matters to him.
157	나에게는 상관없어.
	It doesn't matter to me.
158	이것은 모두에게 중요해.
	It matters to everyone.
159	누군가에게는 중요해.
	It matters to someone.
160	너의 결정이 중요해.
	Your decision matters.

161	너의 의견이 중요해.
	Your opinion matters.
162	더 중요한 건 없어.
	Nothing matters more.
163	크기가 중요한가요?
	Does size matter?
164	시간이 중요한가요?
	Does time matter?
165	돈이 중요한가요?
	Does money matter?
166	나이는 상관없어.
	Age doesn't matter.
167	거리는 상관없어.
	Distance doesn't matter.
168	차 색상은 상관없어.
	The color of car doesn't matter.
169	네가 무엇을 원하건 상관없어.
	Whatever you want doesn't matter.
170	네가 어디를 가건 상관없어.
	Wherever you go doesn't matter.

171	생각보다 훨씬 중요해.
	It matters more than you think.
172	생각보다 덜 중요해.
	It matters less than you think.
173	그게 중요한 거야.
	That's what matters.
174	그래서 그게 중요한 거야.
	That's why it matters.
175	그것이 중요한지 누가 신경 쓰나요?
	Who cares if it matters?
176	가장 중요한 것은 무엇인가요?
	What matters most?
177	인생에서 중요한 것은 무엇인가요?
	What matters in life?
178	그거 중요한 거예요?
	Is it something that matters?
179	언제 가장 중요한가요?
	When does it matter the most?
180	당신에게 중요하기만 하다면.
	As long as it matters to you.

181	얼마나 오래갈까?
	How long will it last?
182	콘서트는 얼마나 했어?
	How long did the concert last?
183	파티 얼마동안 했어?
	How long did the party last?
184	보증 기간은 얼마나 되나요?
	How long does the warranty last?
185	세일은 얼마 동안 할까?
	How long will the sale last?
186	수리가 얼마나 걸릴까?
	How long will the repairs last?
187	이 좋은 날씨가 계속될까?
	Will this good weather last?
188	음식이 내일까지 갈까? (보존될까?)
	Will the food last until tomorrow?
189	이 배터리 더 오래가.
	This battery lasts longer.
190	영화는 거의 세 시간 동안 했어.
	The movie lasted almost three hours.

191	그 교수님 강의 대략 45분간 했어.	
	His lecture lasted about 45 minutes.	
192	토론을 아침 내내 했네.	
	The discussion lasted all morning.	
193	이 모델 5년 동안 유지된 거야.	
	This model lasted for five years.	
194	꽃이 일주일 이상 피어 있었어.	
	The flowers lasted over a week.	
195	여행 2주 동안 했어.	
	The trip lasted two weeks.	
196	통증 몇 일간 계속 있을 거야.	
	The pain will last a few days.	
197	그의 명성은 오래 못 갔어.	
	His fame lasted a short time.	
198	우리의 휴가가 너무 짧게 느껴졌어.	
	Our vacation lasted too short.	
199	그 휴대폰 배터리는 오래 안 가.	
	The phone battery doesn't last long.	
200	그 행복은 오래 가지 않아.	
	That happiness didn't last long.	

Check	
☐	**배터리로 작동하나요?**
	Can it work on battery?
Check	
☐	**저는 마케팅 팀에서 일해요.**
	I work in the Marketing team.
Check	
☐	**일 시작하자.**
	Let's get to work.
Check	
☐	**나는 재택 해.**
	I work from home.
Check	
☐	**아직 일하는 중이야.**
	I'm still at work.
Check	
☐	**그녀는 너무 많이 일해.**
	She works too much.
Check	
☐	**잘 돼요.**
	It works.
Check	
☐	**매번 잘 돼요.**
	It works every time.
Check	
☐	**(일정) 이 일정 나한테 괜찮아요.**
	This works for me.
Check	
☐	**(일정) 그 일정 당신에게 괜찮으시겠어요?**
	Would that work for you?

Check	
☐	**(일정) 월요일 날 괜찮아요.**
	Monday works for me.
Check	
☐	**(식당) 아직 먹고 있어요.**
	I'm working on it.
Check	
☐	**(식당) 아직 드시고 계세요?**
	Are you still working on it?
Check	
☐	**안 돼요.**
	It doesn't work.
Check	
☐	**전혀 안돼요.**
	It never works.
Check	
☐	**지금 안 되는데요.**
	It's not working.
Check	
☐	**지금 안 되나요?**
	Isn't it working?
Check	
☐	**어떻게 하는 거예요?**
	How does it work?
Check	
☐	**그렇게는 안 될 거야.**
	That's not going to work.
Check	
☐	**이게 제일 잘 돼요.**
	This works best.

☐	**나는 매일 일해.** I work every day.
☐	**오늘 밤 늦게까지 일해야 해.** I'm working late tonight.
☐	**점심시간에도 계속 일했어.** I worked through lunch.
☐	**그는 열심히 일하고 있어.** He's hard at work.
☐	**일하러 가야 해.** I'm off to work.
☐	**지금 일하러 가.** I'm heading to work.
☐	**수고하세요.** Keep up the good work.
☐	**수고가 많으세요.** You're doing great work.
☐	**내가 제대로 해볼게. (work on)** I'll work on that.
☐	**제대로 좀 해봐. (work on)** You need to work on it.

Check ☐	**그들이 제대로 일하기 시작했어. (work on)**
	They started working on it.
Check ☐	**저희가 해결하겠습니다. (work out)**
	We'll work it out.
Check ☐	**일이 잘 안 풀려. (work out)**
	It's not working out.
Check ☐	**그들은 잘 어울려.**
	They work well together.
Check ☐	**그거 될까요?**
	Will it work?
Check ☐	**아직도 돼요?**
	Does it still work?
Check ☐	**작동 가능해요.**
	It's workable.
Check ☐	**이거 열심히 했어**
	I worked hard on this.
Check ☐	**일이 바빠.**
	Work's been busy.
Check ☐	**오늘은 일 쉬어요.**
	I'm taking work off today.

Check	
☐	**내일 일해?**
	Are you working tomorrow?
Check	
☐	**그거 중요한 거예요?**
	Is it something that matters?
Check	
☐	**상관없어.**
	It doesn't matter.
Check	
☐	**나이는 상관없어.**
	Age doesn't matter.
Check	
☐	**거리는 상관없어.**
	Distance doesn't matter.
Check	
☐	**차 색상은 상관없어.**
	The color of car doesn't matter.
Check	
☐	**지금은 중요하지 않아.**
	It doesn't matter now.
Check	
☐	**더 이상 중요하지 않아.**
	It doesn't matter anymore.
Check	
☐	**그때는 중요하지 않았어.**
	It didn't matter then.
Check	
☐	**중요해요.**
	It matters.

Check	
☐	**정말 중요해.** It really matters.
☐	**그에게는 중요해.** It matters to him.
☐	**나에게는 상관없어.** It doesn't matter to me.
☐	**매우 중요해.** It matters a lot.
☐	**중요한가요?** Does it matter?
☐	**당신에게 중요한가요?** Does it matter to you?
☐	**갑자기 문제가 됐어.** It suddenly mattered.
☐	**예전에는 많이 중요했어.** It used to matter a lot.
☐	**너의 결정이 중요해.** Your decision matters.
☐	**너의 의견이 중요해.** Your opinion matters.

Check	
☐	**더 중요한 건 없어.**
	Nothing matters more.
Check	
☐	**왜 중요한가요?**
	Why does it matter?
Check	
☐	**얼마나 중요한가요?**
	How much does it matter?
Check	
☐	**무엇이 당신에게 중요한가요?**
	What matters to you?
Check	
☐	**가장 중요한 것은 무엇인가요?**
	What matters most?
Check	
☐	**인생에서 중요한 것은 무엇인가요?**
	What matters in life?
Check	
☐	**크기가 중요한가요?**
	Does size matter?
Check	
☐	**시간이 중요한가요?**
	Does time matter?
Check	
☐	**돈이 중요한가요?**
	Does money matter?
Check	
☐	**이것은 모두에게 중요해.**
	It matters to everyone.

Check	
☐	**누군가에게는 중요해.**
	It matters to someone.
Check	
☐	**그게 중요한 거야.**
	That's what matters.
Check	
☐	**그래서 그게 중요한 거야.**
	That's why it matters.
Check	
☐	**당신에게 중요하기만 하다면.**
	as long as it matters to you.
Check	
☐	**네가 무엇을 원하건 상관없어.**
	Whatever you want doesn't matter.
Check	
☐	**네가 어디를 가건 상관없어.**
	Wherever you go doesn't matter.
Check	
☐	**그것이 중요한지 누가 신경 쓰나요?**
	Who cares if it matters?
Check	
☐	**생각보다 훨씬 중요해.**
	It matters more than you think.
Check	
☐	**생각보다 덜 중요해.**
	It matters less than you think.
Check	
☐	**언제 가장 중요한가요?**
	When does it matter the most?

	그 휴대폰 배터리는 오래 안 가.	
	The phone battery doesn't last long.	
	이 배터리 더 오래가.	
	This battery lasts longer.	
	얼마나 오래갈까?	
	How long will it last?	
	콘서트는 얼마나 했어?	
	How long did the concert last?	
	파티 얼마동안 했어?	
	How long did the party last?	
	보증 기간은 얼마나 되나요?	
	How long does the warranty last?	
	세일은 얼마 동안 할까?	
	How long will the sale last?	
	수리가 얼마나 걸릴까?	
	How long will the repairs last?	
	영화는 거의 세 시간 동안 했어.	
	The movie lasted almost three hours.	
	그 교수님 강의 대략 45분간 했어.	
	His lecture lasted about 45 minutes.	

☐	**토론을 아침 내내 했네.** The discussion lasted all morning.
☐	**이 모델 5년 동안 유지된 거야.** This model lasted for five years.
☐	**꽃이 일주일 이상 피어 있었어.** The flowers lasted over a week.
☐	**여행 2주 동안 했어.** The trip lasted two weeks.
☐	**통증 몇 일간 계속 있을 거야.** The pain will last a few days.
☐	**이 좋은 날씨가 계속될까?** Will this good weather last?
☐	**음식이 내일까지 갈까? (보존될까?)** Will the food last until tomorrow?
☐	**그의 명성은 오래 못 갔어.** His fame lasted a short time.
☐	**우리의 휴가가 너무 짧게 느껴졌어.** Our vacation lasted too short.
☐	**그 행복은 오래 가지 않아.** That happiness didn't last long.

201	**이리 와.**
	Come here.
202	**들어와.**
	Come on in.
203	**나랑 같이 가.**
	Come with me.
204	**나중에 놀러 와. (come over)**
	Come over later.
205	**가까이 와봐.**
	Come closer.
206	**와서 앉아.**
	Come sit down.
207	**내 옆에 앉아.**
	Come sit next to me.
208	**나 찾아 봐라.**
	Come find me!
209	**와서 내가 한 것 좀 봐봐.**
	Come see what I made!
210	**지금 가.**
	I'm coming.

211	나도 같이 가.
	I'm coming with you.
212	지금 바로 갈게.
	I'm coming right away.
213	데리러 갈게.
	I'm coming to pick you up.
214	파티에 갈게.
	I'm coming to the party.
215	와서 봐봐.
	Come and see.
216	와서 드세요.
	Come and get it!
217	우리 집에 놀러 와.
	Come and visit us.
218	와서 나랑 놀아.
	Come and play with me.
219	와서 좀 먹어 봐.
	Come and try some.
220	잠깐만 이리 와 볼래?
	Can you come here for a second?

221	오늘 밤에 갈게. (come over)
	I'll come over tonight.
222	너희 집에 가도 돼? (come over)
	Can I come over to your house?
223	내일 다시 올게요. (come back)
	I'll come back tomorrow.
224	나중에 다시 들르실래요? (come back)
	Can you come back later?
225	언제 올 거야? (come back)
	When will you come back?
226	저녁 먹으러 갈게.
	I'll come for dinner.
227	곧 돌아올게.
	I'll come right back.
228	제가 모시러 갈게요.
	I'll come and get you.
229	이곳에 자주 와.
	I come here often.
230	자전거로 출근해.
	I come to work by bike.

231	매일 배우러 와.
	I come to learn every day.
232	쉬러 왔어.
	I come here to relax.
233	분위기 때문에 와.
	I come for the atmosphere.
234	빨리 와, 영화 시작해.
	Come quick, the movie is starting!
235	안으로 들어가자.
	Let's come inside.
236	너도 왔으면 좋겠어.
	I wish you could come too.
237	자, 이제 네 차례야.
	Come on, it's your turn.
238	제발, 늦겠어.
	Come on, we'll be late!
239	사촌하고 같이 가도 될까? (come along)
	Can my cousin come along?
240	다시 말해 줄래?
	Could you come again?

241	솔직해질 시간이야.
	It's time for you to come clean.
242	보고서 준비해 와.
	Come prepared with your reports.
243	그거 요긴하게 쓰일 거야. (come in handy)
	It may come in handy.
244	그 아이 이제 진짜 성인 됐어. (come of age)
	He has really come of age.
245	그 도시는 밤에 생기가 돌아. (come to life)
	The city comes to life at night.
246	내 친구랑 마주쳤어. (come face to face)
	I came face to face with my friend.
247	독감에 걸린 거 같아. (come down with)
	I think I'm coming down with the flu.
248	그녀는 마라톤에서 첫 번째로 들어왔어. (come in first)
	She came in first in the marathon.
249	둘이 만나서 온 거야? (come together)
	Did you two come together?
250	해결책을 생각해 내야 해. (come up with)
	We need to come up with a solution.

251	이름 한번 지어보자. (come up with)
	Let's come up with a name.
252	뭔데?
	What happened?
253	무슨 일 생긴 거야?
	What just happened?
254	너 무슨 일 있었어?
	What happened to you?
255	무슨 일이야?
	What's happening?
256	늘 그래.
	It happens.
257	그런 일 많아.
	It happens a lot.
258	누구에게나 일어날 수 있어.
	It can happen to anyone.
259	그럴지도 몰라.
	It might happen.
260	절대 그런 일 없을 거야.
	It will never happen.

261	그 일은 일어나지 않았어. It didn't happen.
262	그냥 그렇게 됐어. It just happened.
263	어떻게 된 거야? How did it happen?
264	왜 그런 거야? Why did it happen?
265	얼마나 자주 그런 거야? How often does it happen?
266	어떻게 이런 일이? How could this happen?
267	무슨 일이 있었는지 봤어. I saw what happened.
268	무슨 일이 있었는지 말해 줘. Tell me what happened.
269	큰일 났어. Something big happened.
270	꼭 그렇게 될 거야. It's bound to happen.

271	그런 일은 일어나지 말았어야 했어.
	It shouldn't have happened.
272	무슨 일이 있었는지 잘 모르겠어.
	I'm not sure what happened.
273	원래 자주 그랬어.
	That used to happen.
274	지금도 그래.
	This is happening.
275	저번에 무슨 일 있었어?
	What happened last time?
276	그런 일이 있었어?
	Did it happen?
277	아무 일도 없었어.
	Nothing happened.
278	여전히 그래.
	It still happens.
279	그런 일은 없어.
	That doesn't happen.
280	우리는 어떻게 되는 거야?
	What happens to us?

281	온라인으로 지불해도 되나요?
	Can I pay online?
282	카드로 지불해도 되나요?
	Can I pay by card?
283	현금으로 지불해도 되나요?
	Can I pay in cash?
284	나중에 지불해도 되나요?
	Can I pay later?
285	내 신용카드로 지불할게요.
	I'll pay with my credit card.
286	제때에 지불해 주세요.
	Please pay on time.
287	늦지 않게 지불하는 것을 잊지 마세요.
	Don't forget to pay on time.
288	누가 티켓값 지불할 거야?
	Who will pay for the tickets?
289	현금으로 지불해 주세요.
	Pay in cash, please.
290	선불로 지불해 주세요.
	Pay up front, please.

291	**계산대에서 지불해 주세요.** Please pay at the counter.
292	**따로따로 계산하자.** Let's pay separately.
293	**이제 계산하고 가자.** Let's pay and leave.
294	**너 나 대신 지불했어?** Did you pay for me?
295	**배송 전에 지불해야 해.** You must pay before delivery.
296	**그 일은 수익이 있어.** The job pays.
297	**그 일은 보수가 낮아.** The job pays poorly.
298	**우리 계획 성공할 거야.** Our plan will pay.
299	**너의 일은 보상받을 거야.** Your work will pay.
300	**너의 아이디어는 효과를 볼 거야.** Your idea will pay.

Check	
☐	**지금 가.**
	I'm coming.
☐	**나랑 같이 가.**
	Come with me.
☐	**나도 같이 가.**
	I'm coming with you.
☐	**오늘 밤에 갈게. (come over)**
	I'll come over tonight.
☐	**나중에 놀러 와 (come over)**
	Come over later.
☐	**너희 집에 가도 돼? (come over)**
	Can I come over to your house?
☐	**데리러 갈게.**
	I'm coming to pick you up.
☐	**이리 와.**
	Come here.
☐	**저녁 먹으러 갈게.**
	I'll come for dinner.
☐	**잠깐만 이리 와 볼래?**
	Can you come here for a second?

Check	
☐	**제발, 늦겠어.** Come on, we'll be late!
☐	**분위기 때문에 와.** I come for the atmosphere.
☐	**내 친구랑 마주쳤어. (come face to face)** I came face to face with my friend.
☐	**들어와.** Come on in.
☐	**와서 봐봐.** Come and see.
☐	**와서 드세요.** Come and get it!
☐	**우리 집에 놀러 와.** Come and visit us.
☐	**와서 나랑 놀아.** Come and play with me.
☐	**와서 좀 먹어 봐.** Come and try some.
☐	**가까이 와봐.** Come closer.

Check	
☐	**와서 앉아.**
	Come sit down.
Check	
☐	**내 옆에 앉아.**
	Come sit next to me.
Check	
☐	**와서 내가 한 것 좀 봐봐.**
	Come see what I made!
Check	
☐	**보고서 준비해 와.**
	Come prepared with your reports.
Check	
☐	**나중에 다시 들르실래요? (come back)**
	Can you come back later?
Check	
☐	**언제 올 거야? (come back)**
	When will you come back?
Check	
☐	**내일 다시 올게요. (come back)**
	I'll come back tomorrow.
Check	
☐	**자, 이제 네 차례야.**
	Come on, it's your turn.
Check	
☐	**나 찾아 봐라.**
	Come find me!
Check	
☐	**지금 바로 갈게.**
	I'm coming right away.

Check ☐	**다시 말해 줄래?**	
	Could you come again?	
Check ☐	**파티에 갈게.**	
	I'm coming to the party.	
Check ☐	**곧 돌아올게.**	
	I'll come right back.	
Check ☐	**솔직해질 시간이야.**	
	It's time for you to come clean.	
Check ☐	**자전거로 출근해.**	
	I come to work by bike.	
Check ☐	**매일 배우러 와.**	
	I come to learn every day.	
Check ☐	**너도 왔으면 좋겠어.**	
	I wish you could come too.	
Check ☐	**제가 모시러 갈게요.**	
	I'll come and get you.	
Check ☐	**이곳에 자주 와.**	
	I come here often.	
Check ☐	**쉬러 왔어.**	
	I come here to relax.	

	둘이 만나서 온 거야? (come together)
	Did you two come together?
	빨리 와, 영화 시작해.
	Come quick, the movie is starting!
	안으로 들어가자.
	Let's come inside.
	이름 한번 지어보자. (come up with)
	Let's come up with a name.
	해결책을 생각해 내야 해. (come up with)
	We need to come up with a solution.
	사촌하고 같이 가도 될까? (come along)
	Can my cousin come along?
	그거 요긴하게 쓰일 거야. (come in handy)
	It may come in handy.
	그 아이 이제 진짜 성인 됐어. (come of age)
	He has really come of age.
	그 도시는 밤에 생기가 돌아. (come to life)
	The city comes to life at night.
	독감에 걸린 거 같아. (come down with)
	I think I'm coming down with the flu.

	그녀는 마라톤에서 첫 번째로 들어왔어. (come in first)
	She came in first in the marathon.
	늘 그래.
	It happens.
	그런 일 많아.
	It happens a lot.
	그럴지도 몰라.
	It might happen.
	그 일은 일어나지 않았어.
	It didn't happen.
	절대 그런 일 없을 거야.
	It will never happen.
	원래 자주 그랬어.
	That used to happen.
	지금도 그래.
	This is happening.
	여전히 그래.
	It still happens.
	그냥 그렇게 됐어.
	It just happened.

Check		
☐	**누구에게나 일어날 수 있어.**	
	It can happen to anyone.	
☐	**큰일 났어.**	
	Something big happened.	
☐	**아무 일도 없었어.**	
	Nothing happened.	
☐	**그런 일은 없어.**	
	That doesn't happen.	
☐	**그런 일이 있었어?**	
	Did it happen?	
☐	**무슨 일이야?**	
	What's happening?	
☐	**뭔데?**	
	What happened?	
☐	**무슨 일 생긴 거야?**	
	What just happened?	
☐	**너 무슨 일 있었어?**	
	What happened to you?	
☐	**무슨 일이 있었는지 봤어.**	
	I saw what happened.	

	무슨 일이 있었는지 말해 줘.	
	Tell me what happened.	
	꼭 그렇게 될 거야.	
	It's bound to happen.	
	그런 일은 일어나지 말았어야 했어.	
	It shouldn't have happened.	
	무슨 일이 있었는지 잘 모르겠어.	
	I'm not sure what happened.	
	어떻게 된 거야?	
	How did it happen?	
	왜 그런 거야?	
	Why did it happen?	
	얼마나 자주 그런 거야?	
	How often does it happen?	
	어떻게 이런 일이?	
	How could this happen?	
	저번에 무슨 일 있었어?	
	What happened last time?	
	우리는 어떻게 되는 거야?	
	What happens to us?	

Check	
☐	**내 신용카드로 지불할게요.**
	I'll pay with my credit card.
Check	
☐	**제때에 지불해 주세요.**
	Please pay on time.
Check	
☐	**배송 전에 지불해야 해.**
	You must pay before delivery.
Check	
☐	**늦지 않게 지불하는 것을 잊지 마세요.**
	Don't forget to pay on time.
Check	
☐	**현금으로 지불해 주세요.**
	Pay in cash, please.
Check	
☐	**선불로 지불해 주세요.**
	Pay up front, please.
Check	
☐	**계산대에서 지불해 주세요.**
	Please pay at the counter.
Check	
☐	**그 일은 수익이 있어.**
	The job pays.
Check	
☐	**그 일은 보수가 낮아.**
	The job pays poorly.
Check	
☐	**너 나 대신 지불했어?**
	Did you pay for me?

Check ☐	**온라인으로 지불해도 되나요?**	
	Can I pay online?	
Check ☐	**카드로 지불해도 되나요?**	
	Can I pay by card?	
Check ☐	**현금으로 지불해도 되나요?**	
	Can I pay in cash?	
Check ☐	**나중에 지불해도 되나요?**	
	Can I pay later?	
Check ☐	**우리 계획 성공할 거야.**	
	Our plan will pay.	
Check ☐	**너의 일은 보상받을 거야.**	
	Your work will pay.	
Check ☐	**너의 아이디어는 효과를 볼 거야.**	
	Your idea will pay.	
Check ☐	**따로따로 계산하자.**	
	Let's pay separately.	
Check ☐	**이제 계산하고 가자.**	
	Let's pay and leave.	
Check ☐	**누가 티켓값 지불할 거야?**	
	Who will pay for the tickets?	

PART
2.

2형식 동사로
시작하는
회화 문장

4. 'be'를 활용한 회화 문장(성격, 상태 표현)

301	**행복해.**	
	I'm happy.	
302	**슬퍼.**	
	I'm sad.	
303	**상심했어.**	
	I'm heartbroken.	
304	**화났어.**	
	I'm angry.	
305	**열받네.**	
	I'm upset.	
306	**배고파.**	
	I'm hungry.	
307	**굶어 죽겠어.**	
	I'm starving.	
308	**배불러.**	
	I'm full.	
309	**신나는데.**	
	I'm excited.	
310	**너무 흥분했어.**	
	I'm thrilled.	

311	그 사람 상냥해.
	He's gentle.
312	그 사람 우호적이야.
	He's friendly.
313	그 사람 관대해.
	He's generous.
314	피곤해.
	I'm tired.
315	지친다.
	I'm exhausted.
316	진지해.
	I'm serious.
317	놀랬어.
	I'm surprised.
318	깜짝 놀랐어.
	I'm astonished.
319	실망했어.
	I'm disappointed.
320	무서워.
	I'm scared.

321	**진짜 무섭네.** I'm terrified.
322	**그 여자애 게을러.** She's lazy.
323	**지루해.** I'm bored.
324	**긴장되네.** I'm nervous.
325	**바빠.** I'm busy.
326	**떠나려고.** I'm leaving.
327	**걱정돼.** I'm worried.
328	**만족스러워.** I'm satisfied.
329	**아주 만족해.** I'm content.
330	**혼란스럽네.** I'm confused.

331	짜증 나.
	I'm annoyed.
332	듣고 있어.
	I'm listening.
333	스트레스받아.
	I'm stressed.
334	감사해.
	I'm grateful.
335	걔 되게 덜렁대.
	He's clumsy.
336	외로워.
	I'm lonely.
337	궁금해.
	I'm curious.
338	나 충격받았어.
	I'm shocked.
339	나 망연자실했어.
	I'm devastated.
340	당황스러운데.
	I'm embarrassed.

341	**망신당했어.**
	I'm humiliated.
342	**진짜 기분 나쁘네.**
	I'm offended.
343	**준비됐어.**
	I'm ready.
344	**절박해.**
	I'm desperate.
345	**관심 있어.**
	I'm interested.
346	**관심 없어.**
	I'm not interested.
347	**자신 있어.**
	I'm confident.
348	**그 남자애 질투가 많아.**
	He's jealous.
349	**부럽구나.**
	You are envious.
350	**기뻐.**
	I'm pleased.

351	**즐거워.**
	I'm amused.
352	**아주 기쁜데.**
	I'm delighted.
353	**답답해.**
	I'm frustrated.
354	**목말라.**
	I'm thirsty.
355	**졸려.**
	I'm sleepy.
356	**너 웃겨.**
	You're funny.
357	**간절히 원해.**
	I'm eager.
358	**나 열정적이야.**
	I'm passionate.
359	**나 가난해.**
	I'm poor.
360	**나 비참해.**
	I'm miserable.

361	그는 잘 참아. He's patient.
362	그는 참을성이 없어. He's impatient.
363	너 제정신이 아니야. You're insane.
364	공감하고 있어. I'm sympathetic.
365	그녀가 심드렁하네. She's apathetic.
366	후회해. I'm regretful.
367	억울해. I'm resentful.
368	걔 낙관적이야. He's optimistic.
369	걔 성격이 느긋해. He's easygoing.
370	그녀는 비관적이야. She's pessimistic.

371	그는 거만해.
	He's arrogant.
372	그 여자애 겸손해.
	She's humble.
373	예의 바르네.
	You're polite.
374	무례하네.
	You're rude.
375	정말 못됐어.
	You're so mean.
376	그 사람 정직해.
	He's honest.
377	그 사람 신뢰할 수 있어.
	He's reliable.
378	그는 간사해.
	He's cunning.
379	그녀는 신중해.
	She's thoughtful.
380	그녀는 경계하는 성격이야.
	She's guarded.

381	그 사람 소심해.
	He's timid.
382	그 사람 용감해.
	He's brave.
383	그 사람 무모해.
	He's reckless.
384	그녀는 사랑스러워.
	She's lovely.
385	그녀는 사랑스러워. (주로 아기)
	She's adorable.
386	그녀는 사치스러워.
	She's lavish.
387	그녀는 검소해.
	She's thrifty.
388	그녀는 말이 많아.
	She's talkative.
389	그녀는 과묵해.
	She's reserved.
390	나 자극 받았어.
	I'm motivated.

391	나 영감 받았어.
	I'm inspired.
392	그 사람 야망 있어.
	He's ambitious.
393	그 사람 파이팅이 넘쳐.
	He's energetic.
394	그 사람 외향적이야.
	He's outgoing.
395	그 사람 공격적이야.
	He's aggressive.
396	그 사람 고집 세.
	He's stubborn.
397	그 사람 잘 속아.
	He's gullible.
398	그 사람 귀가 얇아.
	He's easily swayed.
399	그 여자애 예민해.
	She's sensitive.
400	그 여자애 상처 잘 받아.
	She's vulnerable.

Check	
☐	**배고파.** I'm hungry.
☐	**굶어 죽겠어.** I'm starving.
☐	**배불러.** I'm full.
☐	**피곤해.** I'm tired.
☐	**지친다.** I'm exhausted.
☐	**무서워.** I'm scared.
☐	**진짜 무섭네.** I'm terrified.
☐	**진지해.** I'm serious.
☐	**떠나려고.** I'm leaving.
☐	**듣고 있어.** I'm listening.

해당 문장 테스트 ▶▶▶

Check	
☐	**바빠.**
	I'm busy.
Check	
☐	**외로워.**
	I'm lonely.
Check	
☐	**긴장되네.**
	I'm nervous.
Check	
☐	**지루해.**
	I'm bored.
Check	
☐	**신나는데.**
	I'm excited.
Check	
☐	**너무 흥분했어.**
	I'm thrilled.
Check	
☐	**화났어.**
	I'm angry.
Check	
☐	**열받네.**
	I'm upset.
Check	
☐	**슬퍼.**
	I'm sad.
Check	
☐	**상심했어.**
	I'm heartbroken.

Check	
	행복해.
	I'm happy.
	놀랐어.
	I'm surprised.
	깜짝 놀랐어.
	I'm astonished.
	실망했어.
	I'm disappointed.
	만족스러워.
	I'm satisfied.
	아주 만족해.
	I'm content.
	감사해.
	I'm grateful.
	걱정돼.
	I'm worried.
	혼란스럽네.
	I'm confused.
	짜증 나.
	I'm annoyed.

	스트레스받아. I'm stressed.
	궁금해. I'm curious.
	관심 있어. I'm interested.
	관심 없어. I'm not interested.
	자신 있어. I'm confident.
	절박해. I'm desperate.
	간절히 원해. I'm eager.
	나 열정적이야. I'm passionate.
	나 충격받았어. I'm shocked.
	나 망연자실했어. I'm devastated.

Check	
☐	**당황스러운데.**
	I'm embarrassed.
Check	
☐	**망신당했어.**
	I'm humiliated.
Check	
☐	**진짜 기분 나쁘네.**
	I'm offended.
Check	
☐	**준비됐어.**
	I'm ready.
Check	
☐	**기뻐.**
	I'm pleased.
Check	
☐	**즐거워.**
	I'm amused.
Check	
☐	**아주 기쁜데.**
	I'm delighted.
Check	
☐	**답답해.**
	I'm frustrated.
Check	
☐	**그 사람 상냥해.**
	He's gentle.
Check	
☐	**그 사람 우호적이야.**
	He's friendly.

Check	
☐	**그 사람 관대해.**
	He's generous.
Check	
☐	**나 가난해.**
	I'm poor.
Check	
☐	**나 비참해.**
	I'm miserable.
Check	
☐	**후회해.**
	I'm regretful.
Check	
☐	**억울해.**
	I'm resentful.
Check	
☐	**목말라.**
	I'm thirsty.
Check	
☐	**졸려.**
	I'm sleepy.
Check	
☐	**나 자극 받았어.**
	I'm motivated.
Check	
☐	**나 영감 받았어.**
	I'm inspired.
Check	
☐	**공감하고 있어.**
	I'm sympathetic.

Check	**그 사람 정직해.**	
☐	He's honest.	
Check	**그 사람 신뢰할 수 있어.**	
☐	He's reliable.	
Check	**그 사람 잘 속아.**	
☐	He's gullible.	
Check	**그 사람 귀가 얇아.**	
☐	He's easily swayed.	
Check	**그 사람 고집 세.**	
☐	He's stubborn.	
Check	**그 남자애 질투가 많아.**	
☐	He's jealous.	
Check	**부럽구나.**	
☐	You are envious.	
Check	**그 여자애 게을러.**	
☐	She's lazy.	
Check	**그는 잘 참아.**	
☐	He's patient.	
Check	**그는 참을성이 없어.**	
☐	He's impatient.	

☐	**그녀가 심드렁하네.** She's apathetic.
☐	**걔 낙관적이야.** He's optimistic.
☐	**걔 성격이 느긋해.** He's easygoing.
☐	**그녀는 비관적이야.** She's pessimistic.
☐	**너 웃겨.** You're funny.
☐	**너 제정신이 아니야.** You're insane.
☐	**그녀는 사랑스러워.** She's lovely.
☐	**그녀는 사랑스러워. (주로 아기)** She's adorable.
☐	**정말 못됐어.** You're so mean.
☐	**그는 간사해.** He's cunning.

Check	
	걔 되게 덜렁대.
	He's clumsy.
Check	
	그녀는 신중해.
	She's thoughtful.
Check	
	그녀는 경계하는 성격이야.
	She's guarded.
Check	
	그녀는 과묵해.
	She's reserved.
Check	
	그는 거만해.
	He's arrogant.
Check	
	그 여자애 겸손해.
	She's humble.
Check	
	예의 바르네.
	You're polite.
Check	
	무례하네.
	You're rude.
Check	
	그녀는 사치스러워.
	She's lavish.
Check	
	그녀는 검소해.
	She's thrifty.

	그 사람 야망 있어. He's ambitious.
	그 사람 파이팅이 넘쳐. He's energetic.
	그 사람 외향적이야. He's outgoing.
	그 사람 공격적이야. He's aggressive.
	그 사람 소심해. He's timid.
	그 여자애 예민해. She's sensitive.
	그 여자애 상처 잘 받아. She's vulnerable.
	그녀는 말이 많아. She's talkative.
	그 사람 용감해. He's brave.
	그 사람 무모해. He's reckless.

401	**멋져.** It's amazing.
402	**아름다워.** It's beautiful.
403	**늦었어.** It's late.
404	**괜찮아.** It's fine.
405	**좋은데.** It's nice.
406	**흥미로워.** It's interesting.
407	**흥미진진한데.** It's fascinating.
408	**이상해.** It's weird.
409	**진짜야. (찐인데)** It's authentic.
410	**믿을 수 없어.** It's unbelievable.

411	보기 드문 일이야. It's unusual.
412	잘못됐어. It's wrong.
413	받아들일 만해. It's acceptable.
414	필수적이야. It's essential.
415	정상이야. It's normal.
416	비정상이야. It's abnormal.
417	독특해. It's unique.
418	엽기적인데. It's bizarre.
419	뻔해. It's typical.
420	쓸 만해. It's useful.

421	**쓸모없어.**
	It's useless.
422	**도움 돼.**
	It's helpful.
423	**가치 있는 거야.**
	It's valuable.
424	**그만한 가치가 있어.**
	It's worth it.
425	**비싸.**
	It's expensive.
426	**싸.**
	It's cheap.
427	**저렴해.**
	It's affordable.
428	**(가격이) 합당해.**
	It's reasonable.
429	**시끄러워.**
	It's noisy.
430	**조용해.**
	It's quiet.

431	**더러워.**
	It's dirty.
432	**공개적인 거야.**
	It's public.
433	**사적인 거야.**
	It's private.
434	**낡았어.**
	It's old.
435	**한물갔어.**
	It's outdated.
436	**새로워.**
	It's new.
437	**갱신했어.**
	It's updated.
438	**위급해.**
	It's urgent.
439	**선택 사항이야.**
	It's optional.
440	**일상이야.**
	It's routine.

441	드물어. It's rare.
442	흔해. It's common.
443	의무적이야. It's mandatory.
444	매우 중요해. It's critical.
445	재미있어. It's fun.
446	꽉 껴. It's tight.
447	느슨해. It's loose.
448	영업 중입니다. It's open.
449	영업 끝났어요. It's closed.
450	노출됐어. It's exposed.

451	밝아. It's bright.
452	어두워. It's dark.
453	(좋은 의미로) 심상치 않아. It's extraordinary.
454	훌륭해. It's awesome.
455	환상적이네. It's fantastic.
456	끔찍해. It's terrible.
457	최악이야. It's horrible.
458	잘했어. It's excellent.
459	인상적이야. It's impressive.
460	신나는데. It's exciting.

| 461 | 지루해. |
| | It's boring. |

| 462 | 편안해. |
| | It's comfortable. |

| 463 | 불편해. |
| | It's uncomfortable. |

| 464 | 아늑해. |
| | It's cozy. |

| 465 | 공간 여유가 좀 있네. |
| | It's spacious. |

| 466 | 비좁아. |
| | It's cramped. |

| 467 | 엄청 커. |
| | It's enormous. |

| 468 | 거대해. |
| | It's huge. |

| 469 | 사람 없어. |
| | It's vacant. |

| 470 | 사람 있어. |
| | It's occupied. |

471	볼 수 있어. It's visible.
472	볼 수 없어. It's invisible.
473	들을 수 있어. It's audible.
474	들을 수 없어. It's inaudible.
475	만질 수 있어. It's tangible.
476	휴대할 수 있어. It's portable.
477	세련됐어. It's fashionable.
478	촌스러워. It's tacky.
479	간단해. It's simple.
480	쉬워. It's easy.

481	**쉽지 않아. (빡세.)** It's challenging.
482	**복잡해.** It's complicated.
483	**정교해.** It's sophisticated.
484	**사치스러워.** It's luxurious.
485	**논리적이야.** It's logical.
486	**합리적이야.** It's rational.
487	**적합해.** It's suitable.
488	**힘들어.** It's hard.
489	**어려워.** It's difficult.
490	**활용성이 있어.** It's functional.

491	**득이 돼.**	
	It's beneficial.	
492	**애매모호하네.**	
	It's ambiguous.	
493	**유명해.**	
	It's famous.	
494	**악명 높아.**	
	It's infamous.	
495	**만석이에요.**	
	It's full.	
496	**붐벼.**	
	It's crowded.	
497	**유연해. (융통성이 좋아)**	
	It's flexible.	
498	**단단해. (융통성이 없어.)**	
	It's rigid.	
499	**안정적이야.**	
	It's stable.	
500	**불안해.**	
	It's unstable.	

빵빵GO 'RANDOM TEST'

Check	
☐	**가치 있는 거야.** It's valuable.
☐	**그만한 가치가 있어.** It's worth it.
☐	**영업 중입니다.** It's open.
☐	**영업 끝났어요.** It's closed.
☐	**비싸.** It's expensive.
☐	**싸.** It's cheap.
☐	**힘들어.** It's hard.
☐	**어려워.** It's difficult.
☐	**안정적이야.** It's stable.
☐	**불안해.** It's unstable.

Check	
☐	**유명해.**
	It's famous.
☐	**악명 높아.**
	It's infamous.
☐	**낡았어.**
	It's old.
☐	**한물갔어.**
	It's outdated.
☐	**새로워.**
	It's new.
☐	**갱신했어.**
	It's updated.
☐	**정상이야.**
	It's normal.
☐	**비정상이야.**
	It's abnormal.
☐	**꽉 껴.**
	It's tight.
☐	**느슨해.**
	It's loose.

Check	
☐	**편안해.**
	It's comfortable.
Check	
☐	**불편해.**
	It's uncomfortable.
Check	
☐	**시끄러워.**
	It's noisy.
Check	
☐	**조용해.**
	It's quiet.
Check	
☐	**저렴해.**
	It's affordable.
Check	
☐	**(가격이) 합당해.**
	It's reasonable.
Check	
☐	**신나는데.**
	It's exciting.
Check	
☐	**지루해.**
	It's boring.
Check	
☐	**드물어.**
	It's rare.
Check	
☐	**흔해.**
	It's common.

Check	
☐	**공개적인 거야.** It's public.
☐	**사적인 거야.** It's private.
☐	**밝아.** It's bright.
☐	**어두워.** It's dark.
☐	**잘했어.** It's excellent.
☐	**인상적이야.** It's impressive.
☐	**(좋은 의미로) 심상치 않아.** It's extraordinary.
☐	**훌륭해.** It's awesome.
☐	**환상적이네.** It's fantastic.
☐	**공간 여유가 좀 있네.** It's spacious.

Check ☐	**비좁아.**	
	It's cramped.	
Check ☐	**엄청 커.**	
	It's enormous.	
Check ☐	**거대해.**	
	It's huge.	
Check ☐	**볼 수 있어.**	
	It's visible.	
Check ☐	**볼 수 없어.**	
	It's invisible.	
Check ☐	**들을 수 있어.**	
	It's audible.	
Check ☐	**들을 수 없어.**	
	It's inaudible.	
Check ☐	**만질 수 있어.**	
	It's tangible.	
Check ☐	**휴대할 수 있어.**	
	It's portable.	
Check ☐	**간단해.**	
	It's simple.	

Check	
☐	**쉬워.**
	It's easy.
Check	
☐	**쉽지 않아. (빡세.)**
	It's challenging.
Check	
☐	**복잡해.**
	It's complicated.
Check	
☐	**정교해.**
	It's sophisticated.
Check	
☐	**만석이에요.**
	It's full.
Check	
☐	**붐벼.**
	It's crowded.
Check	
☐	**사람 없어.**
	It's vacant.
Check	
☐	**사람 있어.**
	It's occupied.
Check	
☐	**끔찍해.**
	It's terrible.
Check	
☐	**최악이야.**
	It's horrible.

Check	
☐	**진짜야. (찐인데)**
	It's authentic.
☐	**믿을 수 없어.**
	It's unbelievable.
☐	**보기 드문 일이야.**
	It's unusual.
☐	**이상해.**
	It's weird.
☐	**잘못됐어.**
	It's wrong.
☐	**늦었어.**
	It's late.
☐	**괜찮아.**
	It's fine.
☐	**좋은데.**
	It's nice.
☐	**독특해.**
	It's unique.
☐	**엽기적인데.**
	It's bizarre.

Check	
☐	**뻔해.** It's typical.
☐	**아늑해.** It's cozy.
☐	**활용성이 있어.** It's functional.
☐	**촌스러워.** It's tacky.
☐	**세련됐어.** It's fashionable.
☐	**사치스러워.** It's luxurious.
☐	**득이 돼.** It's beneficial.
☐	**합리적이야.** It's rational.
☐	**적합해.** It's suitable.
☐	**논리적이야.** It's logical.

Check	
	애매모호하네.
	It's ambiguous.
	멋져.
	It's amazing.
	아름다워.
	It's beautiful.
	필수적이야.
	It's essential.
	의무적이야.
	It's mandatory.
	선택 사항이야.
	It's optional.
	흥미로워.
	It's interesting.
	흥미진진한데.
	It's fascinating.
	재미있어.
	It's fun.
	유연해. (융통성이 좋아)
	It's flexible.

Check	
☐	**단단해. (융통성이 없어.)**
	It's rigid.
Check	
☐	**노출됐어.**
	It's exposed.
Check	
☐	**위급해.**
	It's urgent.
Check	
☐	**쓸 만해.**
	It's useful.
Check	
☐	**쓸모없어.**
	It's useless.
Check	
☐	**더러워.**
	It's dirty.
Check	
☐	**매우 중요해.**
	It's critical.
Check	
☐	**도움 돼.**
	It's helpful.
Check	
☐	**일상이야.**
	It's routine.
Check	
☐	**받아들일 만해.**
	It's acceptable.

501	여기 정말 놀라워.
	It's amazing here.
502	깨지기 쉬워.
	It's fragile.
503	오늘 밤은 고요하네.
	It's calm outside tonight.
504	혼자 가는 거 위험해.
	It's dangerous to go alone.
505	이 행사에서는 붐벼.
	It's crowded at this event.
506	여기 더럽다.
	It's dirty here.
507	오늘 밤 별을 볼 수 있을 것 같아.
	It's possible to see the stars tonight.
508	가 볼 만해.
	It's worth visiting.
509	지금 시작하기에는 늦어.
	It's late to start now.
510	이례적이지만 흥미로워.
	It's unusual but interesting.

511	밤에는 으스스해.
	It's spooky at night.
512	여기 지루해.
	It's boring here.
513	여기 꽉 찼는데.
	It's full here.
514	이 좌석은 좁아.
	It's tight in this seating.
515	그가 동의할지 모르겠다.
	It's doubtful he will agree.
516	우울한 소식이네.
	It's depressing news.
517	여기 시끄러워.
	It's noisy here.
518	여기 안은 편안해.
	It's comfortable in here.
519	때때로 지루해.
	It's tedious at times.
520	그거 입기에 촌스러워.
	It's tacky to wear that.

521	길 위가 울퉁불퉁해.
	It's rough on the road.
522	그렇게 느끼는 게 정상이야.
	It's normal to feel that way.
523	도서관은 조용해.
	It's quiet in the library.
524	견뎌내기 힘드네.
	It's tough to get through.
525	올라가면서 가팔라져.
	It's steep climbing up.
526	거울처럼 반짝여.
	It's shiny like a mirror.
527	겨울에는 여기 뻔해.
	It's typical here in winter.
528	말도 안 되는 일이 일어났네.
	It's ridiculous what happened.
529	그가 전화하지 않은 것이 이상해.
	It's odd he didn't call.
530	요즘은 일찍 어두워져.
	It's dark out early these days.

531	제시간에 오는 것이 중요해.
	It's important to be on time.
532	오늘 일이 더디네.
	It's slow at work today.
533	아이들 방이 엉망이야.
	It's messy in the kids' room.
534	밤에 잘 안 보여.
	It's hard to see at night.
535	출근 시간에 여기는 바빠.
	It's busy here during rush hour.
536	여기는 안전해.
	It's safe here.
537	여기 누가 담당자인지 명확하지 않아.
	It's unclear who is in charge here.
538	이 장치 사용하기 쉬워.
	It's simple to use this device.
539	설명하기 힘들어.
	It's hard to explain.
540	밖에 어마어마한데.
	It's awesome outside.

541	이전과 달라.
	It's different than before.
542	할인 행사 때는 정신없어.
	It's hectic during the sale.
543	여기서 외식은 비싸.
	It's expensive to eat out here.
544	여기서 길 잃기 쉬워.
	It's easy to get lost here.
545	우리에게 새로운 계획이 있어야 하는 건 확실해.
	It's clear we need a new plan.
546	스몰톡 하려는 거 어색해.
	It's awkward trying to make small talk.
547	경기장은 시끄러워.
	It's noisy in the stadium.
548	공부는 해야 해.
	It's necessary to study.
549	도움 요청하는 건 괜찮아.
	It's okay to ask for help.
550	지금 투자하는 건 위험해.
	It's risky to invest now.

551	폭풍우 때는 무서워. It's scary during the storm.
552	우리 모임 하기에 충분히 넓어. It's spacious enough for our party.
553	매번 이기는 것은 불가능하지. It's impossible to win every time.
554	그럴 때 짜증나. It's annoying when that happens.
555	오늘 회사 지루해. It's boring at work today.
556	젖었을 때는 미끄러워. It's slippery when wet.
557	비가 올 것 같아. It's likely to rain.
558	일어날 가능성이 낮아. It's unlikely to happen.
559	누구나 토론할 수 있어. It's open for debate.
560	그가 도착하지 않은 게 이상해. It's strange he hasn't arrived.

561	여기 밤에는 무서워.
	It's terrifying at night here.
562	출근 시간에는 끔찍해.
	It's terrible during rush hour.
563	성능 뛰어난데.
	It's terrific in performance.
564	주말에는 사무실이 텅 비어 있어.
	It's empty in the office on weekends.
565	보는 것이 흥미진진해.
	It's thrilling to watch.
566	디자인이 시대를 초월했어.
	It's timeless in design.
567	모든 면에서 독특해.
	It's unique in every way.
568	호숫가가 멋져.
	It's wonderful at the lakeside.
569	그 남자가 얼마나 많이 아는지 놀랍네.
	It's surprising how much he knows.
570	더위에 끈적거려.
	It's sticky in the heat.

571	지금 떠나도 좋아.
	It's fine to leave now.
572	이 시기에는 이례적이야.
	It's unusual for this time of year.
573	안이 부드러워.
	It's soft inside.
574	여전히 공사 중이야.
	It's still under construction.
575	박물관에서 인상적이었어.
	It's impressive at the museum.
576	모든 연령에 적합해.
	It's suitable for all ages.
577	숙달하기 까다로워.
	It's tricky to master.
578	여기는 깔끔해.
	It's tidy in here.
579	이 문제 해결하는 건 도전적이야.
	It's challenging to solve this problem.
580	반복하는 건 지루해.
	It's tiresome to repeat.

581	대체로 사소해.
	It's trivial in the grand scheme.
582	계획을 갖는 것이 현실적이야.
	It's practical to have a plan.
583	우리의 요구에 완벽해.
	It's perfect for our needs.
584	약속 어기는 건 잘못된 거야.
	It's wrong to break promise.
585	진하고 풍부해.
	It's thick and creamy.
586	이 더위에 불편하네.
	It's uncomfortable in this heat.
587	바위처럼 단단해.
	It's solid as a rock.
588	그건 자체적으로 특별해.
	It's special in its own way.
589	반응이 빨라.
	It's swift in response.
590	그런 친절은 드물어.
	It's rare to find such kindness.

591	시골은 쾌적해.
	It's pleasant in the countryside.
592	지금은 안정되었어.
	It's stable now.
593	어떻게 진행해야 할지 명확하지 않아.
	It's unclear how to proceed.
594	그들이 말하는 거 사실이야.
	It's true what they say.
595	여기서는 드물어.
	It's scarce around here.
596	화려해.
	It's splendid.
597	앞으로 무엇이 있을지 몰라.
	It's unknown what lies ahead.
598	이 매장에서는 저렴해.
	It's affordable at this store.
599	축제에서는 흥이 넘쳐.
	It's upbeat at the festival.
600	처음에는 혼란스러워.
	It's confusing at first.

Check	
☐	**가 볼 만해.**
	It's worth visiting.
☐	**이례적이지만 흥미로워.**
	It's unusual but interesting.
☐	**깨지기 쉬워.**
	It's fragile.
☐	**여기 시끄러워.**
	It's noisy here.
☐	**우울한 소식이네.**
	It's depressing news.
☐	**그거 입기에 촌스러워.**
	It's tacky to wear that.
☐	**그가 전화하지 않은 것이 이상해.**
	It's odd he didn't call.
☐	**여기는 안전해.**
	It's safe here.
☐	**올라가면서 가팔라져.**
	It's steep climbing up.
☐	**여기 안은 편안해.**
	It's comfortable in here.

Check	
☐	**여기 더럽다.**
	It's dirty here.
Check	
☐	**아이들 방이 엉망이야.**
	It's messy in the kids' room.
Check	
☐	**그가 동의할지 모르겠다.**
	It's doubtful he will agree.
Check	
☐	**도서관은 조용해.**
	It's quiet in the library.
Check	
☐	**오늘 밤은 고요하네.**
	It's calm outside tonight.
Check	
☐	**여기 지루해.**
	It's boring here.
Check	
☐	**젖었을 때는 미끄러워.**
	It's slippery when wet.
Check	
☐	**길 위가 울퉁불퉁해.**
	It's rough on the road.
Check	
☐	**거울처럼 반짝여.**
	It's shiny like a mirror.
Check	
☐	**호숫가가 멋져.**
	It's wonderful at the lakeside.

Check ☐	**여기서 외식은 비싸.** It's expensive to eat out here.
Check ☐	**요즘은 일찍 어두워져.** It's dark out early these days.
Check ☐	**여기 정말 놀라워.** It's amazing here.
Check ☐	**그렇게 느끼는 게 정상이야.** It's normal to feel that way.
Check ☐	**지금 시작하기에는 늦어.** It's late to start now.
Check ☐	**밤에 잘 안 보여.** It's hard to see at night.
Check ☐	**겨울에는 여기 뻔해.** It's typical here in winter.
Check ☐	**제시간에 오는 것이 중요해.** It's important to be on time.
Check ☐	**출근 시간에 여기는 바빠.** It's busy here during rush hour.
Check ☐	**때때로 지루해.** It's tedious at times.

Check	**혼자 가는 거 위험해.** It's dangerous to go alone.
Check	**처음에는 혼란스러워.** It's confusing at first.
Check	**경기장은 시끄러워.** It's noisy in the stadium.
Check	**밤에는 으스스해.** It's spooky at night.
Check	**폭풍우 때는 무서워.** It's scary during the storm.
Check	**우리에게 새로운 계획이 있어야 하는 건 확실해.** It's clear we need a new plan.
Check	**여기 누가 담당자인지 명확하지 않아.** It's unclear who is in charge here.
Check	**어떻게 진행해야 할지 명확하지 않아.** It's unclear how to proceed.
Check	**할인 행사 때는 정신없어.** It's hectic during the sale.
Check	**오늘 일이 더디네.** It's slow at work today.

	여기 꽉 찼는데.
	It's full here.
	이 행사에서는 붐벼.
	It's crowded at this event.
	주말에는 사무실이 텅 비어 있어.
	It's empty in the office on weekends.
	이 장치 사용하기 쉬워.
	It's simple to use this device.
	여기서 길 잃기 쉬워.
	It's easy to get lost here.
	설명하기 힘들어.
	It's hard to explain.
	견뎌내기 힘드네.
	It's tough to get through.
	지금 투자하는 건 위험해.
	It's risky to invest now.
	스몰톡 하려는 거 어색해.
	It's awkward trying to make small talk.
	누구나 토론할 수 있어.
	It's open for debate.

	우리 모임 하기에 충분히 넓어.
	It's spacious enough for our party.
	이 좌석은 좁아.
	It's tight in this seating.
	비가 올 것 같아.
	It's likely to rain.
	밖에 어마어마한데.
	It's awesome outside.
	이전과 달라.
	It's different than before.
	도움 요청하는 건 괜찮아.
	It's okay to ask for help.
	그가 도착하지 않은 게 이상해.
	It's strange he hasn't arrived.
	여기 밤에는 무서워.
	It's terrifying at night here.
	출근 시간에는 끔찍해.
	It's terrible during rush hour.
	성능 뛰어난데.
	It's terrific in performance.

	일어날 가능성이 낮아.
	It's unlikely to happen.
	매번 이기는 것은 불가능하지.
	It's impossible to win every time.
	그럴 때 짜증나.
	It's annoying when that happens.
	디자인이 시대를 초월했어.
	It's timeless in design.
	더위에 끈적거려.
	It's sticky in the heat.
	박물관에서 인상적이었어.
	It's impressive at the museum.
	약속 어기는 건 잘못된 거야.
	It's wrong to break promise.
	여전히 공사 중이야.
	It's still under construction.
	공부는 해야 해.
	It's necessary to study.
	오늘 회사 지루해.
	It's boring at work today.

Check		
☐	**오늘 밤 별을 볼 수 있을 것 같아.**	
	It's possible to see the stars tonight.	
☐	**말도 안 되는 일이 일어났네.**	
	It's ridiculous what happened.	
☐	**보는 것이 흥미진진해.**	
	It's thrilling to watch.	
☐	**안이 부드러워.**	
	It's soft inside.	
☐	**여기는 깔끔해.**	
	It's tidy in here.	
☐	**대체로 사소해.**	
	It's trivial in the grand scheme.	
☐	**숙달하기 까다로워.**	
	It's tricky to master.	
☐	**계획을 갖는 것이 현실적이야.**	
	It's practical to have a plan.	
☐	**진하고 풍부해.**	
	It's thick and creamy.	
☐	**이 더위에 불편하네.**	
	It's uncomfortable in this heat.	

	그건 자체적으로 특별해.	
	It's special in its own way.	
	모든 면에서 독특해.	
	It's unique in every way.	
	반응이 빨라.	
	It's swift in response.	
	여기서는 드물어.	
	It's scarce around here.	
	그런 친절은 드물어.	
	It's rare to find such kindness.	
	이 시기에는 이례적이야.	
	It's unusual for this time of year.	
	바위처럼 단단해.	
	It's solid as a rock.	
	화려해.	
	It's splendid.	
	축제에서는 흥이 넘쳐.	
	It's upbeat at the festival.	
	지금 떠나도 좋아.	
	It's fine to leave now.	

Check	
☐	**우리의 요구에 완벽해.**
	It's perfect for our needs.
Check	
☐	**반복하는 건 지루해.**
	It's tiresome to repeat.
Check	
☐	**그들이 말하는 거 사실이야.**
	It's true what they say.
Check	
☐	**지금은 안정되었어.**
	It's stable now.
Check	
☐	**모든 연령에 적합해.**
	It's suitable for all ages.
Check	
☐	**시골은 쾌적해.**
	It's pleasant in the countryside.
Check	
☐	**이 문제 해결하는 건 도전적이야.**
	It's challenging to solve this problem.
Check	
☐	**앞으로 무엇이 있을지 몰라.**
	It's unknown what lies ahead.
Check	
☐	**이 매장에서는 저렴해.**
	It's affordable at this store.
Check	
☐	**그 남자가 얼마나 많이 아는지 놀랍네.**
	It's surprising how much he knows.

7. 'It's'를 활용한 회화 문장(관용 표현)

601	**좋아. 그렇게 하자.** It's a deal.
602	**식은 죽 먹기야.** It's a breeze.
603	**아주 쉬워.** It's a piece of cake.
604	**말하자면 길어.** It's a long story.
605	**생각할 필요도 없어. (너무 쉬워)** It's a no-brainer.
606	**세상 참 좁네.** It's a small world.
607	**유감이야.** It's a pity.
608	**아쉽네.** It's a shame.
609	**흔한 실수야.** It's a common mistake.
610	**임시방편이야.** It's a quick fix.

611	우연이네.
	It's a coincidence.
612	결정하기 어려워.
	It's a tough call.
613	아슬아슬해.
	It's a close call.
614	다 끝났어!
	It's a wrap!
615	게임 체인저야.
	It's a game changer.
616	생명의 은인이야.
	It's a lifesaver.
617	농담이야.
	It's a joke.
618	엉망이네.
	It's a mess.
619	도전인 거지.
	It's a challenge.
620	배꼽 빠지겠네.
	It's a riot.

621	신나.
	It's a blast.
622	악몽이야.
	It's a nightmare.
623	백일몽이야.
	It's a daydream.
624	우여곡절이 많아.
	It's a roller coaster.
625	실망이야.
	It's a letdown.
626	이거 거저 주는 거네.
	It's a steal.
627	배려 섬세하네.
	It's a nice touch.
628	매우 재미있어.
	It's a hoot.
629	드문 기회야.
	It's a rare opportunity.
630	당연지사야.
	It's a given.

631	골치 아파.
	It's a headache.
632	아수라장이네.
	It's a zoo out there.
633	짜릿해.
	It's a thrill.
634	지루해.
	It's a bore.
635	자주 일어나는 일이야.
	It's a regular occurrence.
636	정말 좋은 아이디어야!
	It's a great idea!
637	꼭 해봐야죠.
	It's a must-try.
638	많은 분들이 고르는 메뉴예요.
	It's a popular choice.
639	힘든 상황이야.
	It's a tough situation.
640	좋은 기회야.
	It's a good opportunity.

641	바쁜 하루네. It's a busy day.
642	좀 과해. It's a bit too much.
643	좀 꽉 끼네. It's a bit tight.
644	개인적인 선택이지 뭐. It's a personal choice.
645	중대한 결정이에요. It's a big decision.
646	진짜 문제네요. It's a real problem.
647	흥미진진한데. It's a funny story.
648	잘 어울려요. It's a good match.
649	좀 이르네요. It's a bit early.
650	환대해주시네요. It's a warm welcome.

651	빡빡한 일정이네.
	It's a tight schedule.
652	간단한 식사야.
	It's a quick meal.
653	큰 실수야.
	It's a big mistake.
654	딱 맞아요.
	It's a perfect fit.
655	조용한 하루네.
	It's a quiet day.
656	진짜 특가예요.
	It's a real bargain.
657	엄청난 성공이야.
	It's a huge success.
658	반가운 변화네.
	It's a welcome change.
659	만석이에요.
	It's a full house.
660	꼭 맞아요.
	It's a tight fit.

661	익숙한 얼굴인데.
	It's a familiar face.
662	안전한 선택이에요.
	It's a safe choice.
663	다행이야.
	It's a relief.
664	자주 일어나는 일이에요.
	It's a regular occurrence.
665	행운의 기회네요.
	It's a lucky break.
666	이건 기적이야.
	It's a miracle.
667	단골들 사이에서 인기 메뉴예요.
	It's a favorite among our regulars.
668	일이 많아.
	It's a lot of work.
669	감당하기 버거워.
	It's a lot to take in.
670	네 차례야.
	It's your turn.

671	저희 우선순위예요.
	It's our priority.
672	처음입니다.
	It's my first time.
673	기쁘네요.
	It's my pleasure.
674	내 잘못이야.
	It's my fault.
675	내 결정이야.
	It's my decision.
676	내가 쏠게.
	It's my treat.
677	다 마음대로 해.
	It's all yours.
678	다 됐습니다.
	It's all set.
679	다 좋아요.
	It's all good.
680	제 입장에서는 다 좋아요.
	It's all good on my end.

681	그게 최선이야.
	It's for the best.
682	그것은 판매용입니다.
	It's for sale.
683	그것은 임대용입니다.
	It's for rent.
684	내가 한턱 쏠게.
	It's on me.
685	서비스입니다.
	It's on the house.
686	입에 맴돌고 있어.
	It's on the tip of my tongue.
687	계속 생각나.
	It's on my mind.
688	오른쪽에 있어.
	It's on the right.
689	왼쪽에 있어.
	It's on the left.
690	세일 중입니다.
	It's on sale.

691	다음 페이지에 있어요.
	It's on the next page.
692	전시 중입니다.
	It's on display.
693	일부러 그런 거야.
	It's on purpose.
694	가고 있잖아.
	It's on the way.
695	모두의 입에 오르내리고 있어.
	It's on everyone's lips.
696	대기 중이야.
	It's on hold.
697	후순위로 밀렸어.
	It's on the back burner.
698	네가 결정해.
	It's up to you.
699	기다릴 만한 가치가 있어.
	It's worth the wait.
700	해 볼 만해.
	It's worth a try.

Check	
☐	**말하자면 길어.**
	It's a long story.
Check	
☐	**아슬아슬해.**
	It's a close call.
Check	
☐	**우연이네.**
	It's a coincidence.
Check	
☐	**게임 체인저야.**
	It's a game changer.
Check	
☐	**농담이야.**
	It's a joke.
Check	
☐	**도전인 거지.**
	It's a challenge.
Check	
☐	**우여곡절이 많아.**
	It's a roller coaster.
Check	
☐	**악몽이야.**
	It's a nightmare.
Check	
☐	**식은 죽 먹기야.**
	It's a breeze.
Check	
☐	**아주 쉬워.**
	It's a piece of cake.

Check	좋아. 그렇게 하자.
☐	It's a deal.

Check	세상 참 좁네.
☐	It's a small world.

Check	진짜 특가예요.
☐	It's a real bargain.

Check	꼭 해봐야죠.
☐	It's a must-try.

Check	배려 섬세하네.
☐	It's a nice touch.

Check	신나.
☐	It's a blast.

Check	내가 한턱 쏠게.
☐	It's on me.

Check	서비스입니다.
☐	It's on the house.

Check	다 좋아요.
☐	It's all good.

Check	제 입장에서는 다 좋아요.
☐	It's all good on my end.

	오른쪽에 있어.	
	It's on the right.	
	왼쪽에 있어.	
	It's on the left.	
	임시방편이야.	
	It's a quick fix.	
	결정하기 어려워.	
	It's a tough call.	
	이거 거저 주는 거네.	
	It's a steal.	
	엉망이네.	
	It's a mess.	
	짜릿해.	
	It's a thrill.	
	지루해.	
	It's a bore.	
	매우 재미있어.	
	It's a hoot.	
	정말 좋은 아이디어야!	
	It's a great idea!	

	생명의 은인이야.	
	It's a lifesaver.	
	처음입니다.	
	It's my first time.	
	기쁘네요.	
	It's my pleasure.	
	내 잘못이야.	
	It's my fault.	
	내 결정이야.	
	It's my decision.	
	내가 쏠게.	
	It's my treat.	
	유감이야.	
	It's a pity.	
	아쉽네.	
	It's a shame.	
	다 끝났어!	
	It's a wrap!	
	좀 과해.	
	It's a bit too much.	

Check	
☐	**좀 꽉 끼네.**
	It's a bit tight.
Check	
☐	**좋은 기회야.**
	It's a good opportunity.
Check	
☐	**흥미진진한데.**
	It's a funny story.
Check	
☐	**진짜 문제네요.**
	It's a real problem.
Check	
☐	**환대해주시네요.**
	It's a warm welcome.
Check	
☐	**생각할 필요도 없어. (너무 쉬워)**
	It's a no-brainer.
Check	
☐	**드문 기회야.**
	It's a rare opportunity.
Check	
☐	**골치 아파.**
	It's a headache.
Check	
☐	**당연지사야.**
	It's a given.
Check	
☐	**배꼽 빠지겠네.**
	It's a riot.

Check	
☐	**바쁜 하루네.**
	It's a busy day.
Check	
☐	**안전한 선택이에요.**
	It's a safe choice.
Check	
☐	**좀 이르네요.**
	It's a bit early.
Check	
☐	**빡빡한 일정이네.**
	It's a tight schedule.
Check	
☐	**다 마음대로 해.**
	It's all yours.
Check	
☐	**다 됐습니다.**
	It's all set.
Check	
☐	**엄청난 성공이야.**
	It's a huge success.
Check	
☐	**익숙한 얼굴인데.**
	It's a familiar face.
Check	
☐	**딱 맞아요.**
	It's a perfect fit.
Check	
☐	**조용한 하루네.**
	It's a quiet day.

Check	
☐	**반가운 변화네.** It's a welcome change.
☐	**기다릴 만한 가치가 있어.** It's worth the wait.
☐	**해 볼 만해.** It's worth a try.
☐	**중대한 결정이에요.** It's a big decision.
☐	**그것은 판매용입니다.** It's for sale.
☐	**그것은 임대용입니다.** It's for rent.
☐	**대기 중이야.** It's on hold.
☐	**후순위로 밀렸어.** It's on the back burner.
☐	**힘든 상황이야.** It's a tough situation.
☐	**실망이야.** It's a letdown.

Check	
☐	**잘 어울려요.**
	It's a good match.
Check	
☐	**다행이야.**
	It's a relief.
Check	
☐	**꼭 맞아요.**
	It's a tight fit.
Check	
☐	**간단한 식사야.**
	It's a quick meal.
Check	
☐	**개인적인 선택이지 뭐.**
	It's a personal choice.
Check	
☐	**자주 일어나는 일이에요.**
	It's a regular occurrence.
Check	
☐	**일이 많아.**
	It's a lot of work.
Check	
☐	**감당하기 버거워.**
	It's a lot to take in.
Check	
☐	**그게 최선이야.**
	It's for the best.
Check	
☐	**네가 결정해.**
	It's up to you.

	입에 맴돌고 있어.
	It's on the tip of my tongue.
	계속 생각나.
	It's on my mind.
	세일 중입니다.
	It's on sale.
	다음 페이지에 있어요.
	It's on the next page.
	전시 중입니다.
	It's on display.
	일부러 그런 거야.
	It's on purpose.
	가고 있잖아.
	It's on the way.
	모두의 입에 오르내리고 있어.
	It's on everyone's lips.
	네 차례야.
	It's your turn.
	저희 우선순위예요.
	It's our priority.

☐	**만석이에요.** It's a full house.
☐	**아수라장이네.** It's a zoo out there.
☐	**큰 실수야.** It's a big mistake.
☐	**백일몽이야.** It's a daydream.
☐	**많은 분들이 고르는 메뉴예요.** It's a popular choice.
☐	**행운의 기회네요.** It's a lucky break.
☐	**이건 기적이야.** It's a miracle.
☐	**자주 일어나는 일이야.** It's a regular occurrence.
☐	**흔한 실수야.** It's a common mistake.
☐	**단골들 사이에서 인기 메뉴예요.** It's a favorite among our regulars.

701	오늘은 맑아.
	It's sunny today.

702	밖이 흐려.
	It's cloudy outside.

703	또 비가 와.
	It's raining again.

704	밖이 정말 더워.
	It's really hot out.

705	오늘은 꽤 춥네.
	It's quite cold today.

706	밖이 쾌적해.
	It's pleasant outside.

707	오늘 아침은 쌀쌀해.
	It's chilly this morning.

708	지금 따뜻해지고 있어.
	It's warming up now.

709	오늘은 얼어붙을 듯이 춥네.
	It's freezing today.

710	지금 바람이 살짝 불어.
	It's breezy right now.

711	점점 따뜻해지고 있어.
	It's getting warmer.
712	오늘 밤에 서늘해져.
	It's cooling off tonight.
713	오늘 저녁은 눅눅해.
	It's damp this evening.
714	오늘은 습해.
	It's humid today.
715	건조하고 덥네.
	It's dry and hot.
716	눈이 많이 와.
	It's snowing heavily.
717	아침에 안개가 자욱하네.
	It's foggy in the morning.
718	도로가 얼었어.
	It's icy on the roads.
719	아주 바람이 세.
	It's very windy.
720	오늘 밤은 맑아.
	It's clear tonight.

| 721 | 이슬비가 내려. |
| | It's drizzling. |

| 722 | 오늘 후텁지근하네. |
| | It's muggy today. |

| 723 | 밖에 타는 듯이 더워. |
| | It's scorching out there. |

| 724 | 오늘 별로 나쁜 날씨는 아니야. |
| | It's not too bad today. |

| 725 | 폭풍우가 몰아치고 있어. |
| | It's stormy. |

| 726 | 비가 억수같이 내려. |
| | It's raining cats and dogs. |

| 727 | 의외로 포근하네. |
| | It's surprisingly mild. |

| 728 | 엄청 더워. |
| | It's extremely hot. |

| 729 | 어제보다 추울지는 모르겠네. |
| | It's not as cold as yesterday. |

| 730 | 밖에 눈부셔. |
| | It's beautiful outside. |

731	밖에 날씨가 몹시 나빠.
	It's nasty out there.
732	오늘은 흐려.
	It's overcast today.
733	산책하기 좋은 날씨야.
	It's perfect weather for a walk.
734	우울한 날씨네.
	It's gloomy.
735	강풍 불어.
	It's blustery.
736	오늘 날씨가 정말 안 좋아.
	It's awful weather today.
737	때 아닌 포근함이네.
	It's unseasonably warm.
738	완벽한 날이야.
	It's a perfect day.
739	더위에 숨이 턱턱 막혀.
	It's stifling in the heat.
740	살짝 춥네.
	It's a bit nippy.

741	어제보다 훨씬 시원해.
	It's much cooler than yesterday.
742	너무 습해.
	It's too humid.
743	화창한 날씨야.
	It's a gorgeous day.
744	비 오기 시작해.
	It's starting to rain.
745	전형적인 봄 날씨네.
	It's typical spring weather.
746	오늘 푹푹 찌네.
	It's a scorcher today.
747	밖에 비가 많이 내리고 있어.
	It's really coming down out there.
748	하이킹하기 딱이네.
	It's ideal weather for hiking.
749	금방이라도 비 올 것 같아.
	It's threatening to rain.
750	밖에 사우나처럼 더워.
	It's like a sauna outside.

751	안개가 짙어지고 있어.
	It's getting foggy.
752	비가 오는 날이야.
	It's a wet day.
753	이맘때는 유난히 더워.
	It's unusually hot for this time of year.
754	비 온 후에는 상쾌해.
	It's refreshing after the rain.
755	약간 쌀쌀하지만 상쾌해.
	It's a little brisk.
756	조금 쌀쌀해.
	It's a tad chilly.
757	숨 막힐 정도로 무더워.
	It's oppressively hot.
758	아름다운 저녁이야.
	It's a lovely evening.
759	좀 축축해.
	It's a bit damp.
760	꽤 큰 폭풍이야.
	It's quite a storm.

761	우박 내려.
	It's hailing.
762	딱 좋은 온도네.
	It's the perfect temperature.
763	약간 흐려.
	It's a bit overcast.
764	찌는 듯 더워.
	It's sweltering.
765	캠핑하기에 좋은 날씨야.
	It's good weather for camping.
766	조금 우울한 날이야.
	It's a bit gloomy.
767	아침에 서리가 내렸어.
	It's frosty this morning.
768	깨끗하고 산뜻해.
	It's crisp and clear.
769	바람이 잔잔해.
	It's a calm day.
770	포근하고 쾌적해.
	It's mild and pleasant.

771	비가 어마어마해. It's absolutely pouring.
772	바람이 조금 세. It's a bit too windy.
773	오늘은 비가 가볍게 내려. It's light rain today.
774	이 계절치고는 좀 덥네. It's pretty warm for this season.
775	약간 이슬비가 내려. It's just drizzling a bit.
776	밖에 날씨가 별로 좋지 않네. It's not very nice out.
777	나들이 가기 좋은 날이야. It's a great day for an outing.
778	밖이 우중충해. It's miserable out.
779	포근해. It's balmy.
780	평소보다 춥네. It's colder than usual.

781	밖이 마치 오븐 같아.
	It's like an oven outside.
782	해변 가기 좋은 날씨야.
	It's the perfect day for the beach.
783	매우 차가운 날씨야.
	It's raw and cold.
784	너무 건조해.
	It's too dry.
785	기분 좋게 시원해.
	It's delightfully cool.
786	거의 얼어붙을 듯해.
	It's almost freezing.
787	반갑게 날씨가 변하네.
	It's a nice change.
788	운전하기 안 좋은 날씨야.
	It's terrible weather for driving.
789	너무 습해서 불편해.
	It's so humid it's uncomfortable.
790	살짝 바람이 불어.
	It's a bit breezy.

791	날씨가 괜찮아.
	It's decent out.
792	오늘 날씨가 오락가락해.
	It's variable today.
793	약간 끈적끈적해.
	It's kind of sticky.
794	비가 양동이로 쏟아지네.
	It's pouring buckets.
795	겨울 왕국 같아.
	It's a winter wonderland.
796	마치 봄 같은 날씨야.
	It's spring-like outside.
797	바람이 차갑고 강해.
	It's brisk and windy.
798	소풍 가기 좋은 날이네.
	It's a lovely day for a picnic.
799	최고의 날씨는 아니야.
	It's not the best weather.
800	수영하기에는 너무 추워.
	It's too chilly for swimming.

Check	
☐	**오늘은 맑아.**
	It's sunny today.
☐	**밖이 쾌적해.**
	It's pleasant outside.
☐	**오늘 밤은 맑아.**
	It's clear tonight.
☐	**의외로 포근하네.**
	It's surprisingly mild.
☐	**산책하기 좋은 날씨야.**
	It's perfect weather for a walk.
☐	**화창한 날씨야.**
	It's a gorgeous day.
☐	**전형적인 봄 날씨네.**
	It's typical spring weather.
☐	**완벽한 날이야.**
	It's a perfect day.
☐	**하이킹하기 딱이네.**
	It's ideal weather for hiking.
☐	**아름다운 저녁이야.**
	It's a lovely evening.

Check	
☐	**딱 좋은 온도네.**
	It's the perfect temperature.

Check	
☐	**캠핑하기에 좋은 날씨야.**
	It's good weather for camping.

Check	
☐	**바람이 잔잔해.**
	It's a calm day.

Check	
☐	**마치 봄 같은 날씨야.**
	It's spring-like outside.

Check	
☐	**지금 따뜻해지고 있어.**
	It's warming up now.

Check	
☐	**점점 따뜻해지고 있어.**
	It's getting warmer.

Check	
☐	**때 아닌 포근함이네.**
	It's unseasonably warm.

Check	
☐	**어제보다 훨씬 시원해.**
	It's much cooler than yesterday.

Check	
☐	**깨끗하고 산뜻해.**
	It's crisp and clear.

Check	
☐	**비 온 후에는 상쾌해.**
	It's refreshing after the rain.

Check ☐	**약간 쌀쌀하지만 상쾌해.** It's a little brisk.
Check ☐	**포근하고 쾌적해.** It's mild and pleasant.
Check ☐	**나들이 가기 좋은 날이야.** It's a great day for an outing.
Check ☐	**포근해.** It's balmy.
Check ☐	**해변 가기 좋은 날씨야.** It's the perfect day for the beach.
Check ☐	**소풍 가기 좋은 날이네.** It's a lovely day for a picnic.
Check ☐	**살짝 바람이 불어.** It's a bit breezy.
Check ☐	**날씨가 괜찮아.** It's decent out.
Check ☐	**기분 좋게 시원해.** It's delightfully cool.
Check ☐	**지금 바람이 살짝 불어.** It's breezy right now.

Check	
☐	**오늘 밤에 서늘해져.** It's cooling off tonight.
☐	**반갑게 날씨가 변하네.** It's a nice change.
☐	**밖이 정말 더워.** It's really hot out.
☐	**오늘 후텁지근하네.** It's muggy today.
☐	**건조하고 덥네.** It's dry and hot.
☐	**밖에 타는 듯이 더워.** It's scorching out there.
☐	**오늘 푹푹 찌네.** It's a scorcher today.
☐	**엄청 더워.** It's extremely hot.
☐	**밖에 사우나처럼 더워.** It's like a sauna outside.
☐	**찌는 듯 더워.** It's sweltering.

	숨 막힐 정도로 무더워.	
	It's oppressively hot.	
	더위에 숨이 턱턱 막혀.	
	It's stifling in the heat.	
	이 계절치고는 좀 덥네.	
	It's pretty warm for this season.	
	밖이 마치 오븐 같아.	
	It's like an oven outside.	
	이맘때는 유난히 더워.	
	It's unusually hot for this time of year.	
	오늘은 꽤 춥네.	
	It's quite cold today.	
	오늘 아침은 쌀쌀해.	
	It's chilly this morning.	
	오늘은 얼어붙을 듯이 춥네.	
	It's freezing today.	
	눈이 많이 와.	
	It's snowing heavily.	
	도로가 얼었어.	
	It's icy on the roads.	

☐	**밖에 날씨가 몹시 나빠.** It's nasty out there.
☐	**아주 바람이 세.** It's very windy.
☐	**폭풍우가 몰아치고 있어.** It's stormy.
☐	**오늘은 흐려.** It's overcast today.
☐	**강풍 불어.** It's blustery.
☐	**살짝 춥네.** It's a bit nippy.
☐	**거의 얼어붙을 듯해.** It's almost freezing.
☐	**겨울 왕국 같아.** It's a winter wonderland.
☐	**바람이 차갑고 강해.** It's brisk and windy.
☐	**수영하기에는 너무 추워.** It's too chilly for swimming.

Check	
☐	**조금 쌀쌀해.**
	It's a tad chilly.
Check	
☐	**평소보다 춥네.**
	It's colder than usual.
Check	
☐	**매우 차가운 날씨야.**
	It's raw and cold.
Check	
☐	**오늘 저녁은 눅눅해.**
	It's damp this evening.
Check	
☐	**좀 축축해.**
	It's a bit damp.
Check	
☐	**오늘은 습해.**
	It's humid today.
Check	
☐	**이슬비가 내려.**
	It's drizzling.
Check	
☐	**비가 억수같이 내려.**
	It's raining cats and dogs.
Check	
☐	**우울한 날씨네.**
	It's gloomy.
Check	
☐	**너무 습해.**
	It's too humid.

Check	
☐	**비 오기 시작해.**
	It's starting to rain.
Check	
☐	**밖에 비가 많이 내리고 있어.**
	It's really coming down out there.
Check	
☐	**금방이라도 비 올 것 같아.**
	It's threatening to rain.
Check	
☐	**비가 오는 날이야.**
	It's a wet day.
Check	
☐	**꽤 큰 폭풍이야.**
	It's quite a storm.
Check	
☐	**우박 내려.**
	It's hailing.
Check	
☐	**약간 흐려.**
	It's a bit overcast.
Check	
☐	**조금 우울한 날이야.**
	It's a bit gloomy.
Check	
☐	**아침에 서리가 내렸어.**
	It's frosty this morning.
Check	
☐	**비가 어마어마해.**
	It's absolutely pouring.

Check	
☐	**바람이 조금 세.**
	It's a bit too windy.
Check	
☐	**오늘은 비가 가볍게 내려.**
	It's light rain today.
Check	
☐	**약간 이슬비가 내려.**
	It's just drizzling a bit.
Check	
☐	**밖에 날씨가 별로 좋지 않네.**
	It's not very nice out.
Check	
☐	**밖이 우중충해.**
	It's miserable out.
Check	
☐	**오늘 날씨가 정말 안 좋아.**
	It's awful weather today.
Check	
☐	**밖이 흐려.**
	It's cloudy outside.
Check	
☐	**또 비가 와.**
	It's raining again.
Check	
☐	**너무 습해서 불편해.**
	It's so humid it's uncomfortable.
Check	
☐	**약간 끈적끈적해.**
	It's kind of sticky.

	비가 양동이로 쏟아지네. It's pouring buckets.
	아침에 안개가 자욱하네. It's foggy in the morning.
	오늘 별로 나쁜 날씨는 아니야. It's not too bad today.
	어제보다 추울지는 모르겠네. It's not as cold as yesterday.
	밖에 눈부셔. It's beautiful outside.
	안개가 짙어지고 있어. It's getting foggy.
	너무 건조해. It's too dry.
	운전하기 안 좋은 날씨야. It's terrible weather for driving.
	오늘 날씨가 오락가락해. It's variable today.
	최고의 날씨는 아니야. It's not the best weather.

801	이 스프는 맛있어.
	The soup is delicious.
802	이 피자는 놀라워.
	The pizza is amazing.
803	이 스테이크는 완벽해.
	The steak is perfect.
804	이 샐러드는 신선해.
	The salad is fresh.
805	이 치킨은 육즙이 많아.
	The chicken is juicy.
806	이 소스는 매워.
	The sauce is spicy.
807	이 빵은 (오래돼서) 퍽퍽해.
	The bread is stale.
808	이 생선은 부드러워.
	The fish is tender.
809	이 파스타는 덜 익었어.
	The pasta is undercooked.
810	이 밥은 고슬고슬해.
	The rice is fluffy.

811	이 소고기는 질겨.
	The beef is tough.
812	이 커피는 진해.
	The coffee is strong.
813	이 차는 너무 달아.
	The tea is too sweet.
814	이 국수는 너무 맛있어.
	The noodles are yummy.
815	이 버거는 느끼해.
	The burger is greasy.
816	이 초콜릿은 진해.
	The chocolate is rich.
817	이 과일은 잘 익었어.
	The fruit is ripe.
818	이 와인은 부드러워.
	The wine is smooth.
819	이 케이크는 촉촉해.
	The cake is moist.
820	이 맥주는 쓴맛이 나.
	The beer is bitter.

821	이 카레는 너무 매워.
	The curry is hot.
822	야채가 아삭아삭해.
	The vegetables are crisp.
823	이 치즈는 꽤 숙성되었어.
	The cheese is quite aged.
824	이 샌드위치는 만족스러워.
	The sandwich is satisfying.
825	이 계란은 지나치게 익혔어.
	The egg is overcooked.
826	이 드레싱은 새콤해. (톡 쏘는 맛)
	The dressing is tangy.
827	이 스무디는 산뜻해.
	The smoothie is refreshing.
828	이 과자 칩은 짜.
	The chips are salty.
829	이 살사는 덩어리가 많아. (씹히는 맛)
	The salsa is chunky.
830	이 요거트는 크리미해.
	The yogurt is creamy.

831	이 스프는 싱거워.
	The soup is bland.
832	이 비빔밥은 맛이 풍부해.
	The bibimbap is flavorful.
833	이 감자튀김은 바삭바삭해.
	The fries are crispy.
834	이 파이는 너무 달아.
	The pie is sugary.
835	이 돼지고기는 훈제 맛이 나.
	The pork is smoky.
836	이 쌀떡은 찰 져.
	The rice cake is sticky.
837	이 아이스크림은 차가워.
	The ice cream is cold.
838	이 수플레는 폭신 폭신해.
	The souffle is fluffy.
839	이 커피는 쓴맛이 나.
	The coffee is bitter.
840	이 그레이비소스는 진해.
	The gravy sauce is thick.

841	이 스튜는 푸짐해.
	The stew is hearty.
842	이 오트밀은 곤죽 같아.
	The oatmeal is mushy.
843	이 차는 향이 좋아.
	The tea is aromatic.
844	이 새우는 너무 익혔어.
	The shrimp is overcooked.
845	이 토스트는 탔어.
	The toast is burnt.
846	이 주스는 톡 쏘는 맛이 나.
	The juice is tangy.
847	이 칵테일은 독해.
	The cocktail is boozy.
848	이 머핀은 건조해.
	The muffins are dry.
849	이 양고기는 즙이 많고 맛있어.
	The lamb is succulent.
850	이 두부는 부드러워.
	The tofu is soft.

851	이 볶음밥은 짭조름해.
	The fried rice is savory.
852	이 팝콘은 버터 맛이 나.
	The popcorn is buttery.
853	이 도넛은 너무 달아.
	The donut is sugary.
854	이 커스터드는 부드러워.
	The custard is smooth.
855	이 피클은 시큼해.
	The pickles are sour.
856	이 베이컨은 바삭바삭해.
	The bacon is crispy.
857	이 칠면조는 건조해.
	The turkey is dry.
858	이 라자냐는 치즈 맛이 나.
	The lasagna is cheesy.
859	이 김치는 마늘 맛이 나.
	The kimchi is garlicky.
860	이 스프는 물이 너무 많아.
	The soup is watery.

861	이 샐러드는 약간 시들었어. The salad is wilted.
862	이 불닭은 매워. The buldak is spicy.
863	이 초콜릿은 진하고 풍부해. The chocolate is decadent.
864	이 페이스트리는 얇게 잘 벗겨져. The pastry is flaky.
865	이 콩은 양념이 되어 있어. The beans are seasoned.
866	이 갈비는 걸쭉해. The ribs are sticky.
867	이 잼은 풍미가 강해. The jam is zesty.
868	이 사과주는 시큼털털해. The cider is tart.
869	이 보드카는 독해. The vodka is strong.
870	이 우유는 상했어. The milk is spoiled.

871	이 죽은 뜨거워.
	The porridge is hot.
872	이 베이글은 씹는 맛이 있어.
	The bagels are chewy.
873	이 가리비는 잘 구워졌어요.
	The scallops are seared.
874	이 요거트는 감미로워.
	The yogurt is lucious.
875	이 케밥은 훈제 맛이 나.
	The kebab is smoky.
876	이 호두파이는 고소해.
	The pecan pie is nutty.
877	이 무스는 가벼워.
	The mousse is light.
878	이 치즈는 향이 강해.
	The cheese is pungent.
879	이 라비올리는 섬세해.
	The ravioli is delicate.
880	이 녹차는 떫어.
	The green tea is astringent.

881	이 스콘은 부서지기 쉬워.
	The scones are crumbly.
882	이 파니니는 바삭해.
	The panini is toasty.
883	이 굴은 비려.
	The oysters are fishy.
884	이 닭날개 요리는 감칠맛이 있어.
	The chicken-wing is savory.
885	이 마쉬멜로우는 쫀득쫀득해.
	The marshmallow is chewy.
886	이 샤베트는 신맛이 나.
	The sorbet is tart.
887	이 팬케이크는 푹신 푹신해.
	The pancakes are fluffy.
888	이 그래놀라는 바삭바삭해.
	The granola is crunchy.
889	이 버섯은 흙 같은 맛이 나.
	The mushrooms are earthy.
890	그 피자는 군침 돌게 해.
	The pizza is mouth-watering.

891	이 덮밥은 감칠맛 나.
	The donburi is umami.
892	이 퐁듀는 치즈 맛 나.
	The fondue is cheesy.
893	이 크럼블은 맛있어.
	The crumble is tasty.
894	이 소스는 마늘 맛 나.
	The sauce is garlicky.
895	이 자몽은 달콤씁쓸해.
	The grapefruit is bittersweet.
896	이 김치찌개는 엄청 매워.
	The kimchi stew is hot.
897	라면이 불었어.
	The ramen is soggy.
898	이 연어는 부드러워.
	The salmon is tender.
899	이 브라우니는 쫀득해.
	The brownies are gooey.
900	이 오래된 해산물은 역겨워.
	The spoiled seafood is yucky.

빵빵GO 'RANDOM TEST'

Check	
☐	**이 국수는 너무 맛있어.** The noodles are yummy.
☐	**이 스프는 맛있어.** The soup is delicious.
☐	**이 비빔밥은 맛이 풍부해.** The bibimbap is flavorful.
☐	**이 크럼블은 맛있어.** The crumble is tasty.
☐	**이 피자는 놀라워.** The pizza is amazing.
☐	**이 스테이크는 완벽해.** The steak is perfect.
☐	**이 샌드위치는 만족스러워.** The sandwich is satisfying.
☐	**그 피자는 군침 돌게 해.** The pizza is mouth-watering.
☐	**이 가리비는 잘 구워졌어요.** The scallops are seared.
☐	**이 과일은 잘 익었어.** The fruit is ripe.

Check	
	이 샐러드는 신선해.
	The salad is fresh.
	야채가 아삭아삭해.
	The vegetables are crisp.
	이 스무디는 산뜻해.
	The smoothie is refreshing.
	이 치킨은 육즙이 많아.
	The chicken is juicy.
	이 양고기는 즙이 많고 맛있어.
	The lamb is succulent.
	이 차는 향이 좋아.
	The tea is aromatic.
	이 버섯은 흙 같은 맛이 나.
	The mushrooms are earthy.
	이 드레싱은 새콤해. (톡 쏘는 맛)
	The dressing is tangy.
	이 주스는 톡 쏘는 맛이 나.
	The juice is tangy.
	이 피클은 시큼해.
	The pickles are sour.

Check	이 사과주는 시큼털털해.
	The cider is tart.
Check	이 샤베트는 신맛이 나.
	The sorbet is tart.
Check	이 차는 너무 달아.
	The tea is too sweet.
Check	이 초콜릿은 진해.
	The chocolate is rich.
Check	이 와인은 부드러워.
	The wine is smooth.
Check	이 파이는 너무 달아.
	The pie is sugary.
Check	이 도넛은 너무 달아.
	The donut is sugary.
Check	이 초콜릿은 진하고 풍부해.
	The chocolate is decadent.
Check	이 생선은 부드러워.
	The fish is tender.
Check	이 과자 칩은 짜.
	The chips are salty.

	이 볶음밥은 짭조름해. The fried rice is savory.
	이 닭날개 요리는 감칠맛이 있어. The chicken-wing is savory.
	이 덮밥은 감칠맛 나. The donburi is umami.
	이 소스는 매워. The sauce is spicy.
	이 불닭은 매워. The buldak is spicy.
	이 카레는 너무 매워. The curry is hot.
	이 김치찌개는 엄청 매워. The kimchi stew is hot.
	이 맥주는 쓴맛이 나. The beer is bitter.
	이 커피는 쓴맛이 나. The coffee is bitter.
	이 보드카는 독해. The vodka is strong.

Check		
☐	**이 커피는 진해.**	
	The coffee is strong.	
Check		
☐	**이 칵테일은 독해.**	
	The cocktail is boozy.	
Check		
☐	**이 버거는 느끼해.**	
	The burger is greasy.	
Check		
☐	**이 팝콘은 버터 맛이 나.**	
	The popcorn is buttery.	
Check		
☐	**이 커스터드는 부드러워.**	
	The custard is smooth.	
Check		
☐	**이 팬케이크는 푹신 푹신해.**	
	The pancakes are fluffy.	
Check		
☐	**이 수플레는 푹신 푹신해.**	
	The souffle is fluffy.	
Check		
☐	**이 밥은 고슬고슬해.**	
	The rice is fluffy.	
Check		
☐	**이 연어는 부드러워.**	
	The salmon is tender.	
Check		
☐	**이 그레이비소스는 진해.**	
	The gravy sauce is thick.	

	이 쌀떡은 찰 져. The rice cake is sticky.
	이 스튜는 푸짐해. The stew is hearty.
	이 요거트는 크리미해. The yogurt is creamy.
	이 케이크는 촉촉해. The cake is moist.
	이 오트밀은 곤죽 같아. The oatmeal is mushy.
	이 두부는 부드러워. The tofu is soft.
	이 갈비는 걸쭉해. The ribs are sticky.
	이 브라우니는 쫀득해. The brownies are gooey.
	이 마쉬멜로우는 쫀득쫀득해. The marshmallow is chewy.
	이 라자냐는 치즈 맛이 나. The lasagna is cheesy.

Check	
☐	**이 퐁듀는 치즈 맛 나.**
	The fondue is cheesy.
☐	**이 치즈는 향이 강해.**
	The cheese is pungent.
☐	**이 잼은 풍미가 강해.**
	The jam is zesty.
☐	**이 녹차는 떫어.**
	The green tea is astringent.
☐	**이 스프는 싱거워.**
	The soup is bland.
☐	**이 스프는 물이 너무 많아.**
	The soup is watery.
☐	**이 파스타는 덜 익었어.**
	The pasta is undercooked.
☐	**이 소고기는 질겨.**
	The beef is tough.
☐	**이 살사는 덩어리가 많아. (씹히는 맛)**
	The salsa is chunky.
☐	**이 감자튀김은 바삭바삭해.**
	The fries are crispy.

Check	
☐	**이 베이컨은 바삭바삭해.**
	The bacon is crispy.
Check	
☐	**이 베이글은 씹는 맛이 있어.**
	The bagels are chewy.
Check	
☐	**이 그래놀라는 바삭바삭해.**
	The granola is crunchy.
Check	
☐	**이 스콘은 부서지기 쉬워.**
	The scones are crumbly.
Check	
☐	**이 파니니는 바삭해.**
	The panini is toasty.
Check	
☐	**이 페이스트리는 얇게 잘 벗겨져.**
	The pastry is flaky.
Check	
☐	**이 돼지고기는 훈제 맛이 나.**
	The pork is smoky.
Check	
☐	**이 케밥은 훈제 맛이 나.**
	The kebab is smoky.
Check	
☐	**이 아이스크림은 차가워.**
	The ice cream is cold.
Check	
☐	**이 머핀은 건조해.**
	The muffins are dry.

	이 칠면조는 건조해. The turkey is dry.
	이 김치는 마늘 맛이 나. The kimchi is garlicky.
	이 소스는 마늘 맛 나. The sauce is garlicky.
	이 콩은 양념이 되어 있어. The beans are seasoned.
	이 죽은 뜨거워. The porridge is hot.
	이 요거트는 감미로워. The yogurt is lucious.
	이 호두파이는 고소해. The pecan pie is nutty.
	이 무스는 가벼워. The mousse is light.
	이 라비올리는 섬세해. The ravioli is delicate.
	이 자몽은 달콤씁쓸해. The grapefruit is bittersweet.

Check	
☐	**이 굴은 비려.**
	The oysters are fishy.
Check	
☐	**이 치즈는 꽤 숙성되었어.**
	The cheese is quite aged.
Check	
☐	**이 계란은 지나치게 익혔어.**
	The egg is overcooked.
Check	
☐	**이 토스트는 탔어.**
	The toast is burnt.
Check	
☐	**이 빵은 (오래돼서) 퍽퍽해.**
	The bread is stale.
Check	
☐	**이 새우는 너무 익혔어.**
	The shrimp is overcooked.
Check	
☐	**이 샐러드는 약간 시들었어.**
	The salad is wilted.
Check	
☐	**이 우유는 상했어.**
	The milk is spoiled.
Check	
☐	**라면이 불었어.**
	The ramen is soggy.
Check	
☐	**이 오래된 해산물은 역겨워.**
	The spoiled seafood is yucky.

10. 'look/feel/seem' 그 외 동사를 활용한 회화 문장

901	**이게 누구야.** Look who's here.	
902	**정신 차려. (또는 근사한데?)** Look at you.	
903	**저것 좀 봐.** Look at that.	
904	**내가 말할 때는 나를 봐.** Look at me when I'm talking to you.	
905	**이렇게 생각해봐.** Look at it this way.	
906	**메뉴 좀 볼 수 있을까요?** Can we look at the menu?	
907	**네가 무엇을 했는지 봐.** Look at what you've done.	
908	**뭐 보는데?** What are you looking at?	
909	**나 쳐다보는 거야?** Are you looking at me?	
910	**왜 나 쳐다봐?** Why are you looking at me?	

| 911 | 여기 좀 봐. |
| | Look over here. |

| 912 | 저기 좀 봐. |
| | Look over there. |

| 913 | 이것 좀 봐줄래? |
| | Can you look this over? |

| 914 | 조심해! |
| | Look out! |

| 915 | 차 조심해! |
| | Look out for cars. |

| 916 | 창밖을 봐. |
| | Look out the window. |

| 917 | 서로를 챙겨. |
| | Look out for each other. |

| 918 | 위 좀 봐. |
| | Look up! |

| 919 | 하늘을 올려다봐. |
| | Look up to the sky. |

| 920 | 별 좀 봐봐. |
| | Look up at the stars. |

921	방 주위를 둘러봐.
	Look around the room.
922	(상점) 그냥 둘러보고 있어요.
	I'm just looking around.
923	걔네들 핑계 찾고 있어.
	They look for excuses.
924	뭐 찾는데?
	What are you looking for?
925	거울을 봐.
	Look in the mirror.
926	내 눈을 봐.
	Look into my eyes.
927	미래를 내다봐.
	Look into the future.
928	조사해 볼게.
	I'll look into it.
929	내 강아지 좀 봐줄 수 있어?
	Can you look after my dog?
930	망원경으로 보세요.
	Look through the telescope.

931	뒤를 봐.
	Look behind you.

932	왼쪽을 봐.
	Look to your left.

933	걸어갈 때는 앞을 봐.
	Look where you're going.

934	가까이 봐봐.
	Look closer.

935	좀 더 자세히 볼래?
	Can you look closer?

936	양쪽을 봐.
	Look both ways.

937	잠깐 다른 곳을 봐.
	Look away for a moment.

938	너 피곤해 보여.
	You look tired.

939	걔네들 행복한가 봐.
	They look happy.

940	나는 괜찮아 보여.
	It looks fine to me.

941	걔네들 항상 바빠 보여.
	They always look busy.
942	그녀는 나이에 비해 젊어 보여.
	She looks young for her age.
943	그녀는 준비가 된 것 같아.
	She looks ready.
944	좋아 보이지 않아.
	It doesn't look good.
945	멋져 보여!
	You look great!
946	걔네들 닮았어.
	They look alike.
947	그녀는 여전해 보여.
	She looks the same.
948	그는 건강해 보여.
	He looks well.
949	그는 달라 보여.
	He looks different.
950	그는 조금 길을 잃은 것 같아.
	He looks a little lost.

951	그는 건강해 보여.
	He looks fit.
952	그들은 만족해 보여.
	They look content.
953	비싸 보여.
	It looks expensive.
954	너무 작아 보여.
	It looks too small.
955	쉬워 보일 수 있어.
	It might look easy.
956	그는 아버지를 닮았어.
	He looks like his father.
957	비가 올 것 같아.
	It looks like rain.
958	여행 기대해.
	Look forward to the trip.
959	주말이 기다려져.
	I'm looking forward to the weekend.
960	만나 뵙기를 고대하고 있습니다. (official)
	I'm looking forward to meeting you.

961	회신 기다리겠습니다. (official)
	I'm looking forward to hearing from you.
962	오늘 기분 좋아.
	I feel great today.
963	오늘 기분 좀 어때?
	How do you feel today?
964	괜찮아?
	Do you feel okay?
965	나도 같은 생각이야.
	I feel the same way.
966	그에게 미안한 기분이야.
	I feel bad for him.
967	오해받는 것 같아.
	I feel misunderstood.
968	휴식이 필요한 것 같아.
	I feel like I need a break.
969	피자가 먹고 싶어.
	I feel like eating pizza.
970	영화 보고 싶어.
	I feel like watching a movie.

971	직장 그만두고 싶어.
	I feel like quitting my job.
972	나에게는 괜찮은 것 같아.
	It seems fine to me.
973	좋은 아이디어인 것 같아.
	It seems like a good idea.
974	일이 많은 거 같아.
	It seems like a lot of work.
975	시간 낭비인 것 같아.
	It seems like a waste of time.
976	비가 올 것 같아.
	It seems like it's going to rain.
977	그 계획 실현 가능한 것 같아.
	The plan seems workable.
978	그거 합리적인 것 같아.
	That seems reasonable.
979	방이 붐비는 것 같아.
	The room seems crowded.
980	그 영화 조금 길었던 것 같아.
	The movie seemed a bit long.

981	무슨 문제인가요? What seems to be the issue?
982	좋은 생각인 것 같아. That sounds like a great idea.
983	정말 신나는 일인 것 같아. That sounds like a blast.
984	그거 참 좋은 생각인데. Sounds like a plan.
985	불안해지는데. I become anxious.
986	그 여자 강해지고 있어. She becomes strong.
987	침착해. You stay calm.
988	예의 지켜. You stay polite.
989	계속 집중하는 중이야. I stay focused.
990	그 사람 긴장하는데. He gets nervous.

991	그 사람 더 나아지고 있어.	
	He gets better.	
992	화나는데.	
	I get angry.	
993	그 사람 지쳐가네.	
	He gets tired.	
994	그 여자 조용히 있어.	
	She remains quiet.	
995	그 여자 흔들림이 없어.	
	She remains steady.	
996	그 사람 얼굴이 빨개져.	
	He turns red.	
997	그 여자 얼굴이 창백해졌어.	
	She turns pale.	
998	그 여자 열광하는데.	
	She goes wild.	
999	멍해.	
	I go blank.	
1000	너 참을성이 없어지고 있어.	
	You grow impatient.	

Check	
☐	**조심해!**
	Look out!
Check	
☐	**차 조심해!**
	Look out for cars.
Check	
☐	**창밖을 봐.**
	Look out the window.
Check	
☐	**서로를 챙겨.**
	Look out for each other.
Check	
☐	**뒤를 봐.**
	Look behind you.
Check	
☐	**왼쪽을 봐.**
	Look to your left.
Check	
☐	**내 눈을 봐.**
	Look into my eyes.
Check	
☐	**미래를 내다봐.**
	Look into the future.
Check	
☐	**조사해 볼게.**
	I'll look into it.
Check	
☐	**이게 누구야.**
	Look who's here.

Check	
☐	**메뉴 좀 볼 수 있을까요?**
	Can we look at the menu?
☐	**네가 무엇을 했는지 봐.**
	Look at what you've done.
☐	**뭐 보는데?**
	What are you looking at?
☐	**나 쳐다보는 거야?**
	Are you looking at me?
☐	**왜 나 쳐다봐?**
	Why are you looking at me?
☐	**위 좀 봐.**
	Look up!
☐	**하늘을 올려다봐.**
	Look up to the sky.
☐	**별 좀 봐봐.**
	Look up at the stars.
☐	**비싸 보여.**
	It looks expensive.
☐	**너무 작아 보여.**
	It looks too small.

Check	
☐	**쉬워 보일 수 있어.**
	It might look easy.
Check	
☐	**내 강아지 좀 봐줄 수 있어?**
	Can you look after my dog?
Check	
☐	**방 주위를 둘러봐.**
	Look around the room.
Check	
☐	**(상점) 그냥 둘러보고 있어요.**
	I'm just looking around.
Check	
☐	**정신 차려. (또는 근사한데?)**
	Look at you.
Check	
☐	**저것 좀 봐**
	Look at that.
Check	
☐	**내가 말할 때는 나를 봐.**
	Look at me when I'm talking to you.
Check	
☐	**이렇게 생각해봐.**
	Look at it this way.
Check	
☐	**거울을 봐.**
	Look in the mirror.
Check	
☐	**망원경으로 보세요.**
	Look through the telescope.

Check ☐	**너 피곤해 보여.**	
	You look tired.	
Check ☐	**걔네들 행복한가 봐.**	
	They look happy.	
Check ☐	**나는 괜찮아 보여.**	
	It looks fine to me.	
Check ☐	**양쪽을 봐.**	
	Look both ways.	
Check ☐	**잠깐 다른 곳을 봐.**	
	Look away for a moment.	
Check ☐	**걔네들 항상 바빠 보여.**	
	They always look busy.	
Check ☐	**그녀는 나이에 비해 젊어 보여.**	
	She looks young for her age.	
Check ☐	**그녀는 준비가 된 것 같아.**	
	She looks ready.	
Check ☐	**멋져 보여!**	
	You look great!	
Check ☐	**여행 기대해.**	
	Look forward to the trip.	

	주말이 기다려져. I'm looking forward to the weekend.
	만나 뵙기를 고대하고 있습니다. (official) I'm looking forward to meeting you.
	회신 기다리겠습니다. (official) I'm looking forward to hearing from you.
	여기 좀 봐. Look over here.
	저기 좀 봐. Look over there.
	이것 좀 봐줄래? Can you look this over?
	걔네들 핑계 찾고 있어. They look for excuses.
	뭐 찾는데? What are you looking for?
	그는 건강해 보여. He looks well.
	그는 달라 보여. He looks different.

Check	
☐	**그는 조금 길을 잃은 것 같아.**
	He looks a little lost.
Check	
☐	**그는 건강해 보여.**
	He looks fit.
Check	
☐	**그들은 만족해 보여.**
	They look content.
Check	
☐	**좋아 보이지 않아.**
	It doesn't look good.
Check	
☐	**가까이 봐봐.**
	Look closer.
Check	
☐	**좀 더 자세히 볼래?**
	Can you look closer?
Check	
☐	**그는 아버지를 닮았어.**
	He looks like his father.
Check	
☐	**비가 올 것 같아.**
	It looks like rain.
Check	
☐	**걔네들 닮았어.**
	They look alike.
Check	
☐	**그녀는 여전해 보여.**
	She looks the same.

☐	**걸어갈 때는 앞을 봐.** Look where you're going.
☐	**피자가 먹고 싶어.** I feel like eating pizza.
☐	**영화 보고 싶어.** I feel like watching a movie.
☐	**직장 그만두고 싶어.** I feel like quitting my job.
☐	**휴식이 필요한 것 같아.** I feel like I need a break.
☐	**오늘 기분 좀 어때?** How do you feel today?
☐	**괜찮아?** Do you feel okay?
☐	**오늘 기분 좋아.** I feel great today.
☐	**나도 같은 생각이야.** I feel the same way.
☐	**그에게 미안한 기분이야.** I feel bad for him.

Check ☐	**오해받는 것 같아.** I feel misunderstood.
Check ☐	**무슨 문제인가요?** What seems to be the issue?
Check ☐	**그 계획 실현 가능한 것 같아.** The plan seems workable.
Check ☐	**그거 합리적인 것 같아.** That seems reasonable.
Check ☐	**방이 붐비는 것 같아.** The room seems crowded.
Check ☐	**그 영화 조금 길었던 것 같아.** The movie seemed a bit long.
Check ☐	**나에게는 괜찮은 것 같아.** It seems fine to me.
Check ☐	**좋은 아이디어인 것 같아.** It seems like a good idea.
Check ☐	**일이 많은 거 같아.** It seems like a lot of work.
Check ☐	**시간 낭비인 것 같아.** It seems like a waste of time.

Check	
☐	**비가 올 것 같아.**
	It seems like it's going to rain.
Check	
☐	**좋은 생각인 것 같아.**
	That sounds like a great idea.
Check	
☐	**정말 신나는 일인 것 같아.**
	That sounds like a blast.
Check	
☐	**그거 참 좋은 생각인데.**
	Sounds like a plan.
Check	
☐	**그 사람 얼굴이 빨개져.**
	He turns red.
Check	
☐	**그 여자 얼굴이 창백해졌어.**
	She turns pale.
Check	
☐	**침착해.**
	You stay calm.
Check	
☐	**예의 지켜.**
	You stay polite.
Check	
☐	**그 사람 긴장하는데.**
	He gets nervous.
Check	
☐	**그 사람 더 나아지고 있어.**
	He gets better.

Check	
☐	**화나는데.** I get angry.
☐	**그 사람 지쳐가네.** He gets tired.
☐	**불안해지는데.** I become anxious.
☐	**그 여자 강해지고 있어.** She becomes strong.
☐	**그 여자 열광하는데.** She goes wild.
☐	**멍해.** I go blank.
☐	**계속 집중하는 중이야.** I stay focused.
☐	**그 여자 조용히 있어.** She remains quiet.
☐	**그 여자 흔들림이 없어.** She remains steady.
☐	**너 참을성이 없어지고 있어.** You grow impatient.